Culture in the Federal Republic of Germany, 1945–1995

German Historical Perspectives Series
General Editors:
Gerhard A. Ritter and Anthony J. Nicholls

Volume I
Population, Labour and Migration in 19th- and 20th-Century Germany
Edited by Klaus J. Bade

Volume II
Wealth and Taxation in Central Europe: The History and Sociology of Public Finance
Edited by Peter-Christian Witt

Volume III
Nation-Building in Central Europe
Edited by Hagen Schulze

Volume IV
Elections, Parties and Political Traditions: Social Foundations of German Parties and Party Systems
Edited by Karl Rohe

Volume V
Economic Crisis and Political Collapse: The Weimar Republic, 1924–1933
Edited by Jürgen Baron von Kruedener

Volume VI
Escape into War: The Foreign Policy of Imperial Germany
Edited by Gregor Schöllgen

Volume VII
German Unification: The Unexpected Challenge
Edited by Dieter Grosser

Volume VIII
Germany's New Position in Europe: Problems and Perspectives
Edited by Arnulf Baring

Volume IX
Western Europe and Germany: The Beginnings of European Integration 1945–1960
Edited by Clemens Wurm

Volume X
The Military in Politics and Society in France and Germany in the Twentieth Century
Edited by Klaus-Jürgen Müller

German Historical Perspectives/XI

Culture in the Federal Republic of Germany, 1945–1995

Edited by
REINER POMMERIN

BERG

Oxford / Washington, D.C.

First published in 1996 by
Berg
Editorial Offices:
150 Cowley Road, Oxford, OX4 1JJ, UK
13950 Park Center Road, Herndon Virginia 22070-605, USA

© Reiner Pommerin

Berg is the imprint of Oxford International Publishers Ltd.

Library of Congress Cataloging-in-Publication Data

A catalogue record for this book is available from the Library of Congress.

British Library Cataloguing in Publication Data

A catalogue record for this book is available from the British Library.

ISBN   1 85973 100 7 (Cloth)
        1 85973 105 8 (Paper)

Typeset by JS Typesetting, Wellingborough, Northants.
Printed in the United Kingdom by TJ Press Ltd, Padstow, Cornwall.

Contents

Editorial Preface

The purpose of this series of books is to present the results of research by German historians and social scientists to readers in English-speaking countries. Each of the volumes has a particular theme which will be handled from different points of view by specialists. The series is not limited to the problems of Germany but will also involve publications dealing with the history of other countries, with the general problems of political, economic, social and intellectual history as well as international relations and studies in comparative history.

We hope the series will help to overcome the language barrier which experience has shown obstructs the rapid appreciation of German research in English-speaking countries.

The publication of the series is closely associated with the German Visiting Fellowship at St Antony's College, Oxford, which has existed since 1965, having been originally funded by the Volkswagen Stiftung, later by the British Leverhulme Trust, by the Ministry of Education and Science in the Federal Republic of Germany, and, starting in 1990, by the Stifterverband für die Deutsche Wissenschaft with special funding from C. & A. Mode Düsseldorf. Each volume is based on a series of seminars held in Oxford, which has been conceived and directed by the Visiting Fellow and organized in collaboration with St Antony's College.

The editors wish to thank the Stifterverband für die Deutsche Wissenschaft for meeting the expenses of the original lecture series and for generous assistance with the publication. They hope that this enterprise will help to overcome national introspection and to further international academic discourse and co-operation.

Gerhard A. Ritter   Anthony J. Nicholls

Foreword

This volume consists of lectures given at a seminar which I organized in 1994 and which was held in Hilary Term between January and March 1995 at St Antony's College Oxford. After the unexpected unification of the two Germanys in 1990, it seemed time to re-examine the specific cultural and intellectual beginnings and changes in Germany after 1945. Anthony J. Nicholls agreed that these topics were of interest for a British public and, once published, for English-speaking readers.

I am very grateful to St Antony's College, its Warden, Lord Dahrendorf, and its Fellows and the entire college's staff for their hospitality. I am also grateful to Anthony J. Nicholls for his hospitality, support and interest. At the TU Dresden, Manuela Uhlmann has been a reliable and well-qualified research assistant and Dana Müller – as usual – put everything together with smooth efficiency.

I dedicate this volume to my friends of Oxford days, 'Capt.' John F. Hillen III, Joseph 'Jay' Jakub, III and Geoffrey R. 'Jeff' Sloan.

Reiner Pommerin

REINER POMMERIN

Some Remarks on the Cultural History of the Federal Republic of Germany

Long before the national state of Germany finally came into existence in 1871, there were Germans who shared a language and a rich common culture. This is the German culture enthusiastically described by Madame de Stael in *De l'Allemagne*, and the so-called *Kulturgemeinschaft* and even more the German *Kulturstaat*. It was, however, much more a state of mind than an actual fact.

For many people in the world the Federal Republic of Germany only obviously seems to be the home of BMW, Mercedes Benz, Porsche and, last but not least, of Bayer's famous Aspirin. And numerous English-language books fill the stacks of Oxford's Bodleian Library on the Federal Republic as a major economic and political power in Europe. Jakob Burckhardt thought culture was on the same level of effectiveness in history as state and religion, even rating culture as the true driving force in history.[1] But while the Federal Republic of Germany regards itself as a true *Kulturnation*[2] and in 1995 looks upon culture as a very special and important part of its identity, English-language books on the history of the intellectual and cultural developments in Germany after 1945 are not to be found in the catalogues of either the British Museum or Washington's Library of Congress.

But if one looks into the *Deutsche Bibliographie* (German Bibliography) one is also brought to realize that in the Federal Republic itself only one major and convincing effort has been made so far to write a cultural history of Germany after the Second World War. This is *Die Kulturgeschichte der Bundesrepublik Deutschland*, in three

1

volumes, by Hermann Glaser.[3] Glaser, the former *Kulturreferent* (Cultural Commissioner) of the city of Nuremberg, is well known, particularly for the development of the concept of 'social culture' in the 1970s and 1980s. But so far only the first volume of his work has been translated into English.[4]

Two books of Jost Hermand, a professor of German literature who teaches in the United States, *Kultur im Wiederaufbau – Die Bundesrepublik Deutschland 1945–1965*[5] and *Die Kultur der Bundesrepublik*[6] are also of some help, if one wants to find out more about arts, film, literature, music and theatre in post-war Germany. My edited volume, *The American Impact on Postwar Germany*,[7] contains an examination of the American influence, which extended to all levels of culture and into many aspects of daily life and mass consumption.

Some other publications do concentrate more on aspects of the cultural policy of the Federal Republic or of the different *Länder* governments,[8] and quite a few books have been published on theoretical aspects of culture, mostly by sociologists.[9]

Kultur und Politik in der DDR 1945–1990 is the title of a study by Manfred Jäger.[10] It concentrates on the cultural life of the other part of Germany, the GDR, and the book of Joachim-Rüdiger Groth, *Widersprüche. Literatur und Politik in der DDR 1949–1989*[11] deals with the influence of the SED on the GDR's literature. If one is interested in the SED's official definition of culture one should read Joachim Streisand's *Kultur in der DDR*.[12]

The *Längerfristigen Wechselwirkungen zwischen kultureller und wirtschaftlicher Entwicklung* (the relations between cultural and economic developments) in the Federal Republic are analysed by Marlies Hummel and Karl-Heinz Brodbeck.[13] This book contains much interesting information and many statistics, for example on people who work in the field of culture in Germany, or on the average income of artists. There are of course numerous books which describe the different sectors of everyday cultural life in the Federal Republic, such as theatre, literature, music, film or painting. An interesting first survey of this field is given by *Kultur*, one of the three paperback readers on *Die Bundesrepublik Deutschland* edited by Wolfgang Benz.[14] It also should be remarked that the famous *Geschichte der Bundesrepublik Deutschland* in five volumes edited by Karl Dietrich Bracher, Theodor Eschenburg, Joachim C. Fest und Eberhard Jäckel also includes many remarks dealing with intellectual and cultural developments after 1945.[15]

I.

It does indeed make no sense to look at the cultural developments in the Federal Republic of Germany only after the Republic itself came into existence in 1949. The years that passed between the surrender of 7–9 May 1945 and 10 May 1949, when the *Parlamentarische Rat* (Parliamentary Council) produced the new basic law for the Republic, were of great importance for later developments in the cultural field and for its organization, even if the Germans themselves only had a very limited influence on their course at the very beginning. Many Germans, confronted with political and moral catastrophe, explained it by referring to the interruption of tradition and culture by National Socialism. It seemed therefore necessary to recall the cultural achievements of the Germans, so that they might face up to the future. Culture was a means to educate and stabilize the Germans, which is why cultural life was accorded such a high importance.

One might have imagined that, in the time right after the war, when average Germans had pressing material needs for food, clothing and roofs over their heads, it would have been difficult to get people with many other problems to think of culture. But the opposite was the case, and a look at this crucial time is therefore fascinating and also necessary to understand what happened later in the Republic's everyday cultural life.

It may not really be surprising to see that for the new start of their political and cultural life the Germans went back to the German classics, with a certain preference, of course, for Goethe. Already in 1919 in the *Rat der Volksbeauftragten* (Provisional Government) it was seriously discussed whether the seat of the capital should not be removed from Prussia and Berlin and set up in the south of Germany. One suggestion was to shift the capital of the German Reich to Weimar, the city of Goethe. The idea that the *Nationalversammlung*, the constitutional body of the future republic, should meet at Weimar was ostensibly based on the argument that it would be a good start for the German Republic to convene in the city of Goethe. The real reason was, however, that Weimar could only be reached from Berlin by rail. When demonstrators were expected from the capital this railway could easily be controlled by the police. Also Weimar in the shape of its theatre provided a convention hall big enough for the *Nationalversammlung*.[16]

The return to Goethe, 'the great healer', was suggested in 1946 by the writer Frank Thiess in his essay *Heimkehr zu Goethe* (Getting back to Goethe).[17] The philosopher Eduard Spranger demanded that Germany should in the future turn back to humanism, and referred her to Goethe's writings as the best source of counsel.[18] In Albert Erich Brinkmann's book *Geist im Wandel* it was again Johann Wolfgang von Goethe who supplied the basis for a project of overcoming totalitarianism, re-individualization and a return to humanism.[19] Last but not least, the historian Friedrich Meinecke suggested the foundation of Goethe Societies in all German cities. In these Goethe Societies the ideal of a very personal and individual education should be achieved, to avoid, as Meinecke wrote, the 'pressure of the masses'. Each Sunday the societies should meet to listen to the music of great German composers or to read the writings of great German writers such as Schiller, Rilke and, of course, Goethe.[20] Leo Baeck, disparaging Meinecke's book *jämmerlich* (miserable) wrote in a letter to Theodor Heuß 'Goethe wurde der Mann für die stillen Stunden unter der mit dem Schirm bedeckten Lampe, leider, leider, und daher so oft die Zukunft für die moralischen Drückeberger, leider, leider' ('Goethe became the man for quiet hours under the shaded lamp and, alas, so often pointed the way for those who would evade their moral duty; alas, alas!').[21]

But close to Goethe's Weimar had stood the infamous concentration camp at Buchenwald. Without doubt one has to understand Meinecke's suggestion as one of the many contemporary attempts by the Germans to cope with the horrible fact of mass murder and genocide and to make sure it would never happen again. Theodor Adorno questioned if it could ever be possible to come back to normal life and if it would ever be possible to write poems after Auschwitz. When Thomas Mann visited Germany and Weimar in 1949 he, of course, spoke about *Goethe und die Demokratie* (Goethe and Democracy), but did not even try to visit Buchenwald, which was again serving as a concentration camp, this time for people who were fighting the second totalitarian regime on German soil, the GDR.

II.

The days immediately after the Second World War were terrible days. They were terrible days for so many reasons. The full enormity of the Nazi crimes – the holocaust, the extermination of Russian prisoners and of political enemies, the brutalities committed in reprisal against the guerilla forces in occupied territories – sickened the British Occupation Forces.[22]

For a while all activities in the cultural field were initiated not by the Germans but by the four Allied victors in the war, occupying the country and dividing it into their zones of occupation. Culture was used as part of the re-education programme of the Allies, which attempted to change fundamentally the values, attitudes, and civic character of the Germans.

Cultural activities in Germany between 1933 and 1945 had been centralized – initiated and controlled, in a manner very different from the old German tradition – by the National Socialist central government in Berlin. Never before in German history had there been in Germany a centralization and monopolization of authority in cultural policy. Cultural activities used to be initiated and controlled in early modern times, in the Holy Roman Empire, first of all by the Church and then also by the aristocracy and the big independent cities and later, after the modern state came into existence in the seventeenth and eighteenth centuries, by the numerous states on German territory. It was only in the *Kulturkampf* in the 1880s that Bismarck was able to push the church aside and attain control, especially over the school and university system, which became an instrument of public policy. But still there had never been a centralized control or administration by the government of the German Reich in the field of culture. This continued to be exercised, owing to the federal system, by the different states, by the *Länder*. In the constitution of the Weimar Republic the *Reichsregierung*, the central government, received very limited new powers in the field of culture; for example over schools and universities, and in the new field of foreign cultural policy.

But the National Socialists, in their attempt to concentrate all power within the central government and to limit the power and political influence of the *Länder*, stopped this cultural federalism. The so-called *Kulturschaffenden* – that meant everyone working as an artist, a writer, an actor or a musician – were forced to become members of one of the seven chambers of the *Reichskulturkammer*. Poets and writers, for example, who wanted to continue writing had to be members of the *Reichsschrifttumskammer*. One had to be a true believer in the National Socialist ideology and, of course, very important for the Nazis, of Aryan descent. The ministry for

Volksaufklärung und Propaganda under Josef Goebbels co-ordinated and controlled, with the help of the *Reichskulturkammer*, all cultural activities of the 'Third Reich'. To work officially in the field of culture one had to share the views of the National Socialist Party and to subordinate one's work to the aims of the Nazi state. This was the totalitarian cultural policy. Other competences in the sphere of cultural policy were organized and controlled by the newly created Ministry for Science and Education, the *Reichsministerium für Wissenschaft, Erziehung und Volksbildung*.

If the Allied Nations of the anti-Hitler coalition wanted to be successful in their attempts to democratize and denazify Germany, then they had to get rid of these centralized structures in the field of education and culture.

Law No. 1 of the Allied Government therefore ended the centralization and control of cultural life, and the so-called *Kulturhoheit* was returned to the *Länder* level. The 'Parliamentary Council' accepted this change in the basic law of 1949 and the *Kulturhoheit* remained with the *Länder*. In addition, some fundamental principles of cultural policy were adopted in the basic law itself, as article 5 shows, and also in the constitutions of the *Länder*. The new 1991 constitution of Saxony is the latest example of this approach. Cultural life was protected against the encroachments of the various governments. But the governments themselves functioned as comprehensive promoters of culture, and culture played an important role in their budgets.

Cultural life in Germany of course had its centre, especially in the 1920s, in the capital of the Reich, in Berlin, which at the same time was also the capital of Prussia, Germany's biggest state. But for the greater part of their history the Germans had not been dominated and ruled by a central government. Instead, German history had been determined by the very many smaller or middle-sized states, and therefore there had always been quite a number of places in Germany of cultural importance. Not only Berlin, but also cities like Munich, Nuremberg, Dresden, Leipzig, Cologne, Karlsruhe, Frankfurt or Hamburg, just to mention a few, had provided a life rich in cultural activities.

From that perspective the four zones of occupation only anticipated the concept of federalism of the Federal Republic. In the American Zone for example, the reconstruction of the *Land* of Bavaria brought back into existence an old and traditional German state with a rich cultural life. On the other hand, owing to the dissolution of Prussia, newly created *Länder* such as North-Rhine-Westphalia had a much more difficult task in finding their own cultural identity.

After the abolition of the authority of the central government in the field of culture, there followed a screening of the people who had worked during the Nazi period in the print media, radio, publishing houses, museums, libraries and theatres. Quite a number of artists, scientists and writers had emigrated from Germany, but, apart from the ones who had chosen what Frank Thiess called the *Innere Emigration*, the rest obviously had had no difficulties in working for the Third Reich. Some people were dismissed, public libraries were purged of their Nazi literature; in bookshops and publishing houses this literature went off the shelves. Up to the present books from the time of the Third Reich are still on blacklists in the libraries of German universities, and only available for academic research. Nazi literature such as Adolf Hitler's *Mein Kampf* cannot of course to this day be printed or sold in Germany. Unfortunately plenty of Nazi propaganda material from the rich Nazi organizations in the United States, Canada or even Britain now finds its way to the small group of Neo-Nazis in Germany.

III.

While bookstores and libraries were still suffering from the loss of stocks, the printing of new books was very limited at the beginning. German book production, which had been leading the world in 1932, shrank between 1945 and 1947 to a tenth of its former volume. In the American Zone, reading rooms and the so-called *Amerikahäuser* opened, and provided the Germans mostly with American literature. For the British Zone of Germany the Political Intelligence Division created a Book Selection Committee. This Committee recommended titles to be translated and printed in the British Zone. Both the English classics and contemporary writing were made available in the English language in the Source Libraries, the British Council libraries and most of all the reading rooms of *Die Brücke*.

Literature in the English language had only a limited appeal for German publishers. But while the German reader longed mostly for escapist literature, fiction and novels, the Allies were above all aiming with their literature to consolidate humanitarian and democratic attitudes. The German literary journals of the time suggested a strong desire for discussion of contemporary issues. It should be questioned, though, whether that was perhaps only the desire and wish of some of their reviewers and critics, rather than reflecting the views of the average German. However, American and French literature, as a look into the literary journals between 1945 and 1950 shows, seemed to the book reviewers much more relevant than English literature, with which most German readers had already been acquainted before the war, while with American and French literature there was more need to catch up with new titles. Only after 1949 did the number of British books translated into German and published by German publishers increase to a certain degree. Owing to the fact that English became the most important foreign language for the Federal Republic, there were and still are a greater number of books sold in the English language. Authors like Ernest Hemingway, William Saroyan, and Thomas Wolfe found their German readers, as well as André Gide, Albert Camus and Jean-Paul Sartre and Graham Greene and Evelyn Waugh.

Like the publishing houses, which mostly published translated American literature in editions of 5000, the newspapers remained under the control of the Allied military administrations until 1949. Before 1948, they only came out two or three times a week due to the shortage of paper. The decision to license only four or five big newspapers for the whole of Germany, but a considerably larger number for specific regions, turned out to be decisive for the structure of newspapers in Germany even today. The United States and the USSR more or less dominated the everyday cultural life and activities of this period in Germany, while Great Britain and France remained quietly reserved. One should, however, mention at this point that the work of the British Military Government proved, finally, to be crucial for the reshaping of the political mentality of the Germans, helping them to understand and accept democratic values and institutions.[23]

Beginning in May 1945, in each of the four occupation zones, one major newspaper was printed. *Die Neue Zeitung* for the American, *Die Welt* for the British, the *Nouvelles de France* for the French and the *Tägliche Rundschau* for the Soviet Zone. In addition to that some regional newspapers were licenced. A very important role was played in this field by the 'US Publicity and Psychological Warfare Division', run for a while by the German writer Hans Habe, who had came back to Germany as a an American cultural officer.

An attempt was made to bring back the writers and artists who had emigrated during the time of the Nazi regime. Some of them, like Hans Habe, came back in Allied uniforms, as cultural officers, helping to rediscover 'the other Germany', which had never ceased to exist. Some emigrants, like the writers Hermann Hesse and Thomas Mann, refused to come back and live again in Germany.

Another aim of the cultural policy of the Allies was the rehabilitation of artists, musicians and authors who had been condemned by the Third Reich, whose pictures and sculptures had been called *entartet* (depraved), whose books had been burned publicly and whose music could not be played. These were authors like Thomas Mann and his brother Heinrich Mann, Fritz Werfel and Berthold Brecht, and painters like Max Beckmann, Erich Heckel, Emil Nolde, Otto Dix and Karl Schmitt Rottluff. Music of composers such as Igor Stravinsky, Paul Hindemith and Carl Orff was played again. The Allies, especially the Americans, tried to bring developments in modern art, theatre, literature and music to the attention of the Germans, who had been cut off from international cultural life since 1933.

The Allied broadcasting services acted as pioneers for music at a time when most of the theatres and cinemas had been destroyed. Already on 4 May 1945, *Radio Hamburg*, a station of the Allied Military Government, had started its programmes. Only a short time later the Germans could listen to stations run by the 'Psychological Warfare Division' in Frankfurt, Munich and Stuttgart. The American Forces Network (AFN) transmitted from Bremen. The *Nordwestdeutsche Rundfunk* initiated on 26 September 1946, following a demand from the Germans, its programmes for the British Occupation Zone.[24] Berlin had two radio stations, the American *RIAS Berlin* and until 1956 the *Berliner Rundfunk* of the Soviets. It took until 1955 before the Federal Republic finally managed to get back its broadcasting sovereignty and Germany had its own national broadcasting system. Owing to the organization of the broadcasting services by the Allies and the fact that this organization lasted for such a long time, there was, until the end of the 1980s, only a government-controlled broadcasting system in the Federal Republic. At the end of the 1980s some private broadcasting stations were able to obtain a licence. But most of the ones that started transmitting during the last five years will be lucky to survive, especially if they only concentrate on one city and not, like for example *Antenne Bayern*, on an entire region. The existing radio and television structures of the western part of Germany were also transferred to the east of Germany after unification in 1990.

In 1952 the NWDR in Hamburg started a two-hour television experiment, and from 1 October 1956 the *Tagesschau*, a news programme, could be watched all over Germany, for those who could afford a still quite expensive television set. Owing to the late introduction of television, going to the movies remained a kind of a cultural event in the Federal Republic for a long time.[25]

> Part of the immediate post-war cultural rehabilitation of Germany was to find expression in the film; on the other hand, cinemas are bricks and mortar, and had suffered as extensively from the bombing as any other property [. . .] In Hamburg, principal city in the British Zone, 20 of the pre-war 80 cinemas were in operation early 1946. The great and most significant exception to this was Berlin [. . .] In January 1946 no fewer than 170 cinemas were functioning in Berlin – 56 in the Eastern sector, as compared with the 48 in the American, 38 in the British, and 28 in the French sectors.[26]

The Allies, especially the United States, had no interest in supporting the development of a competitive German film industry, fearing the loss of a potential market in West Germany. They therefore only licenced a few smaller German film-production companies, and it took until 1950 before Germany was allowed to reprivatize the formerly government-run UFI Film Company. It was not until 1953 that a new law finally made it possible to use the money of the former UFI, which had grown larger under the Allied administration, to subsidize the small private film enterprises. The reprivatization started no earlier than 1956, with the establishment of the *Bavaria-Filmkunst AG*. This was at a time when the German market was more or less already dominated by foreign, mostly American, productions.

Starting in 1957 the number of cinema tickets sold shrank continuously, and the same was true for the number of cinemas. The reason was obviously the competition with the new television. Facing the huge numbers of foreign productions, the German film industry could therefore convince the Federal Government of the need to guarantee its German outputs. These bank guarantees turned out to be sheer subsidization. But the German movie business did not profit from these subsidies; new concepts were still awaited.

Only for a short period did some movies such as Helmut Käutner's *In jenen Tagen* try to get to grips with the Nazi past, while others tried to deal with the problems of the present, like the fate of the millions of refugees and homecoming soldiers (100,000 Soldiers had to wait until 1956, 11 years after the end of the war, before they were released from the Soviet Union). The favourite movies of the 1950s and early 1960s provided light entertainment. The Germans, faced with the rebuilding of their destroyed cities and industry, were hardworking people and did not want to be bothered with problems in their movies. They were looking instead for escapist entertainment, enabling them to forget their everyday life. The so-called *Heimatfilm* was the hit of the 1950s and 1960s. The scripts were based on novels of writers like Ludwig Ganghofer, Peter Rosegger and Theodor Strom. The scene was always beautiful southern Bavaria, always with the Alps in the background. And of course love always proved to be the winning force, overcoming all the confusions of the world, and there was always, unlike real life where the rate of divorce increased tremendously, a happy end. Sonja Ziemann and Rudolf Prack were the lovers in the films of the 1950s. Everyday life and politics were not matters for film scripts. *Schwarzwaldmädel* ('The Girl from the Black Forest'), the first such movie in colour, is a perfect example of this type of film.

Other films found their stories going a long way back into German history. *Der Kongreß tanzt* described the 'happy days' of the Congress of Vienna, 1815. The series of *Sissi-Films* starring the very young Romy Schneider, or the movie *Schinderhannes* with Lilo Pulver and O.W. Fischer, were also big commercial successes. Movies like *U 47, Kapitanleutnant Prien*, whose submarine had made its way into Scapa Flow, or the *Stern von Afrika* ('The Star of Africa') the story of the young fighter pilot Joachim Marseille, who had crashed in Africa, and last but not least the series of the *08/15* movies based on the books of Hans Hellmuth Kirst were quite popular with the former soldiers of the Second World War. They showed the war with some humour from the perspective of the average soldier, without any heroic tenor. But all these commercial successes could not prevent the German movie industry from sliding more and more into a major crisis.

In the middle of the 1960s the German movie came to new life and success. A new generation of directors took over. Alexander von Kluge's film *Abschied von Gestern*, criticizing everyday life in the Federal Republic, was the first, only to be followed by Ulrich Schamoni's *Schonzeit für Füchse*, Jean-Marie Straub's *Nicht versöhnt* and Volker Schlöndorff's *Der junge Törless* ('The Young Törless'). But these films, although they won many prizes in foreign countries, were not accepted by the German customers, who did not want criticism of their lives. Finally, between 1969 and 1982 the German movie scene was dominated by Rainer Werner Faßbinder, whose film *Die Ehe der Maria Braun* (The Marriage of Maria Braun) became in 1979 a big international success.

It may also be of some interest to have a look at the development of the post-war German theatre, which, especially in the eyes of the American Military Government, was of high importance. They thought the Germans to be a *Kulturnation* in whose development the theatre had played a crucial role. Only three weeks after the end of the war the *Renaissance-Theater* in Berlin opened with the *Raub der Sabinerinnen*. Between June and December 1945 Berlin, a city in ruins, saw the premières of 121 plays. More than 60 American plays had been translated into the German language – mostly entertaining plays like comedies or detective stories. However, Eugene O'Neill's *Mourning becomes Electra* (*Trauer muß Elektra tragen*), Thornton Wilder's *Wir sind noch einmal davongekommen*, Tennessee Williams's *A Streetcar Named Desire* (*Endstation Sehnsucht*), and *The Glass Menagerie* (*Die Glasmenagerie*) proved to be very popular and successful on German stages. But the biggest hit of that time was Carl Zuckmayer's *Des Teufels General*, which, after some worries of the US Military Government that it was too realistic, was finally staged in summer 1947.

Gustav Gründgens, the former director of the *Staatstheater* in Berlin, was rehabilitated in summer 1946 because he had helped and supported Jewish actors and the wives of Jewish actors during the Third Reich. He decided, as did Heinz Hilpert, the former director of the *Deutsches Theater* in Berlin, not to go back to Berlin, but went to his native town Dusseldorf instead. Hilpert went first to Frankfurt, then to Koblenz and after that to Göttingen. Their decisions not to go back to work in Berlin marked an important new trend in Germany's post-war theatre life. Before 1945 Berlin had been the top place for directors, stage managers and actors. From now on Berlin never again became the centre of the German theatre scene. Berlin, Hamburg, Bremen, Bochum, Dusseldorf, Cologne, Frankfurt, Munich and Stuttgart have ranked since then on the same level. Moving from Berlin to a theatre in these cities was no longer seen as a decline or a demotion. A unique position at that time was held by the *Schauspielhaus* in Zurich. Here all the plays of the first post-war years were first staged, before they came to Germany.

Bertold Brecht's *Dreigroschenopfer* was soon on stage again, while Brecht himself withheld plays like *Courage, Galileo, Der gute Mensch von Sezuan*, and *Puntila* from Germany, even though they had already been on stage in Zurich. He wanted to bring them out in his own interpretation in East Berlin, where he, like some other artists and writers, had moved instead of West Germany.

The currency reform in 1948 saw quite a few private theatres close down.[27] From 115 their number shrank to 31. But most of the theatres run by the cities or funded by the *Länder* were quickly reconstructed – 20 of the former 45 theatres – and another 54 were newly built. The theatres in Mannheim, Cologne and Gelsenkirchen are just three examples of these new modern buildings. The new theatres seem also to have stimulated the customers. Until the end of the 1960s an average of 75 to 80 per cent of theatre seats were regularly sold out. Most of them were bought by subscribers coming not only from the cities themselves but also, by organized bus tours, from the countryside around the cities. The development of most theatres was dominated by their directors. Names like Gründgens in Dusseldorf and Hamburg, Oscar Fritz Schuh in Berlin, Cologne and Hamburg, Hans Schalla in Bochum, and Karl Heinz Stroux in Dusseldorf made theatre history.

In the 1960s many theatre directors like Peter Palitzsch in Stuttgart, Peter Stein in Berlin and Peter Zadek in Bochum tried to combine reality, art and politics on the stage. Martin Walser's *Der schwarze Schwan* ('The Black Swan') or Rolf Hochhuth's *Guerillas* were only two of the hotly debated new plays. Some liked the new trend, others obviously not. The number of theatre tickets sold shrank from 20 to 17 million. At the same time, owing to rising costs (mainly salaries) the financial support from the cities and *Länder* for their theatres rose from 380 million to 1.48 billion marks, causing to this day a never-ending discussion about the justification for such a special subsidy for this small part of Germany's rich cultural life.

IV.

A major controversy had broken out in the meantime over the claim that the *Niveaukultur* or *Hochkultur* of the 1950s and 1960s was much too far away from the everyday life of the Germans.[28] So far only the classic forms of theatre and ballet, of literature and music had been accepted as serious cultural forms. Everything else fell into the category of *Kitsch*. Culture had been during the last twenty years mostly unpolitical. Now the so-called 'socioculture', which had been brought up in discussions during the student rebellion in 1968, wanted to complement the old *Hochkultur*.[29] The problem for the advocates of the new 'socioculture' was that nearly all the money going into the field of culture came from local or regional governments. It was therefore taxpayers' money, and it proved to be very difficult to convince the members of local parliaments to spend money to bring culture to the suburbs.

'Culture for all', as Hilmar Hoffmann, at that time the *Kulturreferent* (Cultural Commsssioner) of the city of Frankfurt wrote,[30] or 'Culture as a civic right', as Hermann Glaser, the *Kulturreferent* (Cultural Commissioner) of the city of Nuremberg demanded,[31] created fascinating activities like the sociocultural centre *KOMM* in Nuremberg. Places like this offered a unique place for numerous cultural activities of the so-called 'free cultural groups'. These groups, some of them amateurs, brought new life and excitement into the suburbs, and drew the attention of many people who had not been attracted by the cultural activities of their cities, which usually offered opera houses, theatres and museums.

These suburban activities were also relatively inexpensive. In the city of Frankfurt for example, twelve activities of the so-called 'alternative culture', subsidized with 420,000 marks, attracted twice as many visitors as the city theatre, subsidized to the tune of 75 million marks. Almost every German city had (and still has) its cultural 'summer programme', with free music and theatre in parks and market-places. Even more popular became the visits to museums and 'special exhibitions'. Visitors numbered 13.9 million in 1970, 35.3 million in 1980 and 73.8 million in 1990. This boom led also to an increase in the number of museums.The number of museums rose from 501 in 1970 to 805 in 1980 and to an unbelievable 2,622 in 1990.

But to face facts, 'socioculture' never was as much subsidized as the *Hochkultur* of the local theatres, exhibitions and opera houses. In a *Land* like North Rhine-Westphalia the cities with more than 50,000 inhabitants spent 1.5 billion marks for their culture in a year, but only 9.9 million for 'sociocultural' events, a meagre 0.6 or 0.8 per cent.

The private sponsoring and fund-raising which provides the main source of income for cultural institutions in the United States, for example, has never been popular in the Federal Republic. The figures for 1992 show that only 360 million marks were donated for cultural events by German industry. This is only four per cent of what is given by the local, regional or federal governments.[32] In total in 1989, for example, 9.7 billion marks were spent by the various governments on culture. Cities and smaller towns spent 57.9 per cent of this sum, the *Länder* spent 40.3 per cent and the Federal Government 1.7 per cent.

During the last two years a new discussion has started to define what German culture should be all about, to consider multiculturalism and what kind of cultural activities should be subsidized in the future with taxpayers' money. A new definition of culture seems, as Dieter E. Zimmer has written in *Die Zeit*, inevitable at a time when a barbecue at a *Stadtsparkasse* (savings bank) is announced as a cultural event.[33] But before this discussion became intense, the costs of unification, of clearing up the mess forty years of a totalitarian communist regime have left behind in the east of Germany, in the field of culture as elsewhere, caught the interest of the public.

The GDR used to maintain about 15,000 libraries, some of them of course very small in size. It had 65 theatres, 87 major orchestras and 751 museums, not to mention the 805 cinemas and 117 zoological establishments and public gardens. It also maintained 8,566 'Youth Clubs'. Owing to the fact that all this had been financed and very efficiently controlled by the central government of the GDR, which in reality was bankrupt, the unification treaty guaranteed financial support for cultural institutions from the Federal government until 1995, knowing that the cities and the five new *Länder* in the East were not, and actually are not to this day, able to pay for this variety of cultural activities, which of course were mostly used to educate the people of the GDR in the true spirit of the Marxist ideology.

Today about 66 per cent of the budget for culture provided by the Federal Government to the new *Länder* is to make sure that most of the theatres and orchestras do not close down. But the impact of unification and new administration on cultural life in the eastern part of Germany cannot yet be foreseen. All in all, unification has enlarged and added tremendously to the cultural life of the old Federal Republic. Dresden, the city where I teach and live, is just a marvellous example. It is obvious that the financial support necessary for the East provided by the taxpayer from the West of Germany – some 138 billion DM last year and equivalent sums in the future – will cause a new discussion on the future course of the cultural policy of the Federal Republic of Germany.

Notes

1. See the definition of 'Kulturgeschichte' by Heide Wunder, 'Kulturgeschichte, Mentalitätengeschichte, Historische Anthropologie', in Richard von Dülmen (ed.), *Fischer Lexikon Geschichte*, Frankfurt am Main 1990, pp. 65–86, at p. 69.
2. See for instance Der Staatsminister beim Bundeskanzler, Anton Pfeifer, 'Ziele der Auswärtigen Kulturpolitik des vereinten Deutschland', in *Bulletin des Presse- und Informationsamts der Bundesregierung*, No. 8, 17 January 1992, pp. 53–6.
3. Hermann Glaser, *Kulturgeschichte der Bundesrepublik Deutschland*, 3 vols, Munich 1983.
4. Hermann Glaser, *The Rubble Years: The Cultural Roots of Postwar Germany*, New York 1986.
5. Jost Hermand, *Kultur im Wiederaufbau. Die Bundesrepublik Deutschland 1945–1965*, Munich 1986.
6. Jost Hermand, *Die Kultur der Bundesrepublik Deutschland 1965–85*, Munich 1988.
7. Reiner Pommerin (ed.), *The American Impact on Postwar Germany*, Providence/Oxford 1995.
8. See for example Manfred Abelein, *Die Kulturpolitik des Deutschen Reiches und die Bundesrepublik Deutschland. Ihre verfassungsrechtliche Entwicklung und ihre verfassungsrechtlichen Probleme*, Cologne/Opladen 1968; Erna Heckel, *Kulturpolitik in der Bundesrepublik von 1949 bis zur Gegenwart*, Cologne 1987.
9. See for example Helmut Brackert and Fritz Wefelmeyer (eds), *Naturplan und Verfallskritik. Zu Begriff und Geschichte der Kultur*, Frankfurt am Main 1984; see also Helmut Brackert and Fritz Wefelmeyer (eds), *Kultur. Bestimmungen im 20. Jahrhundert*, Frankfurt am Main 1990.
10. Manfred Jäger, *Kultur und Politik in der DDR 1945–1990*, Cologne 1995.
11. Joachim Rüdiger Groth, *Widersprüche. Literatur und Politik in der DDR 1949–1989*, Berne/Berlin/Frankfurt am Main 1994.
12. Joachim Streisand, *Kultur in der DDR. Studien zu ihren historischen Grundlagen und ihren Entwicklungsetappen*, East Berlin 1981.
13. Marlies Hummel and Karl-Heinz Brodbeck, *Längerfristige Wechselwirkungen zwischen kultureller und wirtschaftlicher Entwicklung*, Berlin 1991.
14. Wolfgang Benz, *Die Bundesrepublik Deutschland. Geschichte in drei Bänden, Bd. 3: Kultur*, Frankfurt am Main 1983.
15. Karl Dietrich Bracher, Theodor Eschenburg, Joachim C. Fest and

Eberhard Jäckel (eds), *Geschichte der Bundesrepublik Deutschland*, 5 vols, Stuttgart – Mannheim 1983–1987.

16. Reiner Pommerin, *Die Alliierten, die Deutschen und die Hauptstadtfrage nach 1945*, Cologne 1986, p. 9.

17. Frank Thiess, 'Heimkehr zu Goethe', *Nordwestdeutsche Hefte*, 1946, 1, pp. 29–32.

18. Eduard Spranger, 'Stirb und werde!', *Die Sammlung* (Göttingen), 1, 1946, Vol. 7, pp. 389–94.

19. Albert Erich Brinkmann, *Geist im Wandel*, Munich, 1947.

20. Friedrich Meinecke, *Die Deutsche Katastrophe*, Berlin 1946, p. 126.

21. Deutschlands Erneuerung 1945–1950, *Antiquariatskatalog Cobet*, 30, April 1985, No. 245.

22. Lord Annan, *How Dr. Adenauer Rose Resilient From The Ruins of Germany*, The 1982 Bithell Memorial Lecture, Institute of German Studies, University of London 1983.

23. Donald Cameron Watt, *Britain Looks Back to Germany. British Opinion and Policy towards Germany since 1945*, London 1965, pp. 92–8.

24. Hugh Greene, 'Rebuilding German Broadcasting', in Hugh Greene, *The Third Floor Front: A View of Broadcasting in the Sixties*, London 1969, pp. 42–57.

25. See Friedrich P. Kahlenberg, 'Film', in *Die Bundesrepublik Deutschland. Geschichte in drei Bänden, Bd. 3: Kultur*, Frankfurt am Main 1983, pp. 358–96.

26. Roger Manvell and Heinrich Fraenkel, *The German Cinema*, London 1971, p. 102.

27. See Frank-Lothar Kroll, 'Kriegsende und Neubeginn am Rhein. Zur Entwicklung des Bonner Kulturlebens in der Besatzungszeit 1945–1948', in Reiner Pommerin (ed.), *Bonn zwischen Kriegsende und Währungsreform*, Bonn 1991, pp. 35–69.

28. Gerhard Schulze, *Die Erlebnisgesellschaft. Kultursoziologie der Gegenwart*, Frankfurt am Main – New York 1992.

29. See Albrecht Göschel, *Die Ungleichzeitigkeit in der Kultur. Wandel des Kulturbegriffs in vier Generationen*, Schriften des deutschen Instituts für Urbanistik, Stuttgart – Berlin – Cologne 1991.

30. Hilmar Hoffmann, *Kultur für Alle. Perspektiven und Modelle*, Frankfurt am Main 1979 and Hilmar Hoffmann, *Kultur für morgen*, Frankfurt am Main 1985.

31. Hermann Glaser and Karl Heinz Stahl, *Bürgerrecht Kultur*, Frankfurt am Main – Berlin – Vienna 1983.

32. Ifo Institut für Wirtschaftsforschung, 'Neuere Entwicklungen bei der Finanzierung von Kunst und Kultur durch Unternehmen', in *ifo Schnelldienst*, Nos 4 and 5, Munich 1992, pp. 8–23.

33. Dieter E. Zimmer, 'Kultur ist alles. Alles ist Kultur. Über die sinnlose Erweiterung des Kulturbegriffs- und was dies bedeutet für die öffentlichen Etats', in *Die Zeit*, 4.12.1992, p. 67.

HERMANN GLASER

1945 – Cultural Beginnings: Continuity and Discontinuity

In Berlin, the last Philharmonic concert before the end of the Hitler regime took place on 15 April 1945; on the programme were compositions of Beethoven and Wagner. The first concert of the Philharmonic Orchestra after the unconditional surrender was organized on 26 May with works by Mendelssohn, Mozart and Tchaikovsky. In Munich, 70 days after the war had ended the Philharmonic Orchestra conducted by Eugen Jochum had its first concert with works by Mendelssohn, Mozart and Tchaikovsky. Cultural beginnings! Discontinuity prevailed: the heroic music of the *Götterdämmerungs-Zeit* was supplanted by music of Jewish and Russian composers; Mozart was included to prove that the Germans were able to appreciate playful serenity. In autumn, Beethoven, but not yet Wagner, returned to German concert programmes. The past had been easily overcome: the denazification of concert programmes had been completed before the denazification of the Germans by the Allied forces began.

I.

In actual fact German music did not need denazification, although Wagner's anti-Semitism should have been part of the *Trauerarbeit* (task of mourning). From the very beginning of cultural life in the occupation zones of Germany discontinuity and continuity were contradictory elements of the same structure, often hardly to be separated from each other. When, for example, most of the

19

universities were reopened in the year 1945, hardly any of the official speakers mentioned the dubious role the arts had played in the Third Reich, serving as an aesthetic facade for barbarism, or the moral corruption of German universities (beginning in 1933). When on 6 November the University of Hamburg was reopened, Senator Landahl gave a speech, appealing to 'the best of this heavily afflicted nation' and to the 'glory of the eternally youthful Hansa city of Hamburg' in order to stress once again 'the German share in Western culture, to the honor of the immortal German spirit'. 'On this occasion of the solemn reopening of the University of Hamburg, which was once and will be again no more and no less than a rebirth out of a new spirit, our first thoughts must be of the students of every university and college from the Old World and the New who, during the six-year struggle of the people of this earth, found their deaths on battlefields and oceans around the world. Their life was still beginning, irradiated with the power of idealism that inspires every young man. It ended early, their mothers, young wives, and fiancées have shed and will continue to shed tears for some time to come.'[1] It was not asked who had been responsible for the catastrophe!

The official language of that time – being an important indicator of cultural consciousness – shows that, despite the break with an authoritarian mentality the 'old' pathos still dominated. As well as formal and political language, literary language lacked what might be called the realistic–dialectic approach to the world of phenomena. During his newspaper work, Hans Habe, the editor of the outstanding American newspaper for Germany, *Die Neue Zeitung*, noticed that apparently only a few German journalists remained untouched by the bacillus of Nazi language. 'One of the best German journalists brought me an excellent article in which he denounced the language of the inhuman creature, asking for the return to *true* German language. It was the excellent article of a man with the best of intentions, and yet, we were not able to print it because it was written in Hitler German.' What, however, constituted 'Hitler German' could not easily be determined. If one disregarded the content, the same pathos was used in the time of dictatorship as it was under a democracy. In November 1945, Dolf Sternberger began his column *Aus dem Wörterbuch des Unmenschen* ('From the Dictionary of the Inhuman') in the first issue of the journal *Die Wandlung*. This series, in which Gerhard Storz and W.E. Süskind were also involved, continued for three years. Its intention was to point out and to eradicate, through language analysis, the degeneration of words and concepts in the Third Reich. A democratic language, as the articulation of human attitude and morality, was to replace the artificial sentence structure, stunted grammar, and monstrous and crippled vocabulary expressive of despotism. Among others, the following words were denounced: *Anliegen* (request); *Ausrichtung* (alignment); *Betreuung* (control); *charakterlich* (of character); *durchführen* (carry through); *Einsatz* (involvement); *Frauenarbeit* (women's work); *Gestaltung* (shaping); *Kulturschaffende* (those creating culture); *Lager* (camp); *leistungsmässig* (concerning efficiency); *Mädel* (girl); *Menschenbehandlung* (treatment of people); *organisieren* (to organize); *Propaganda* (propaganda); *Schulung* (Training); *Vertreter* (representative) and *Zeitgeschehen* (current affairs).

II.

The 'belief in the eternity of the cultural and spiritual world' also remained unquestioned and unchallenged by the new educational policies developed for secondary schools after Germany's collapse. While Theodor W. Adorno, living in exile in the USA, in his *Minima moralia* noted that German culture had completely failed, and one might also remember a saying of Franz Grillparzer: the German mind would take its path from humanity via nationalism to barbarism, these educational schemes were essentially a flight of idealistic fancy which regarded neither facts and reality nor the historic situation. There was no awareness of the German cultural perversion: that the German mind, with its remarkable contributions to world culture in the fields of philosophy, literature, fine arts and music, had been instrumentalized by nationalistic ideology in the nineteenth and twentieth centuries. With regard to schools, for example, textbooks had tried to suppress the Enlightenment and the humane components of the idealistic and romantic movements for generations of pupils and students. Friedrich Nietzsche, himself prone to authoritarian thinking, was an ardent critic of what he called the devastation of the German spirit in favour of the German Reich, while Schopenhauer thought that the German petit-bourgeois class was like a flock of sheep following an ass. To cut the long story of the perversion of the German mind short: *Spießer-Ideologie* (philistine ideology) had dominated German official cultural policy and cultural life for decades (especially since the days of the Second Reich). Herbert Marcuse called it the victory of affirmative culture – a culture that assisted, and justified the misdeeds, and later even the terror, of the ruling class.

The philistine is not conscious of culture – yet he considers himself the wellspring of the nation's culture. His sense of art is permeated by barbarism; war and art, vulgarity and beauty become interchangeable concepts; he is not conscious of this schizophrenia; the split personality is the essence of the philistine. The Goethe he reveres resembles the soldier king; beauty is admired, but it is actually nakedness; purity is advocated but it is sterile purity; the exalted phrases he speaks are empty; the ideals he strives for are really the *Spießer's* (philistine) idols; the avenue to inwardness is littered with sentimental journalism; the tunes he sings are trash, the revered myth is colportage; and the tenderness towards home suffocates in velour. It was that aesthetification of barbarism which culminated in Hitler and his movement. A commentary on Hitler's *Mein Kampf*, an examination of its anthropological, sociological and psychological contents shows that this book was nothing but a mish-mash of trends arising chiefly from the misinterpretation of Classicism and Romanticism during the nineteenth century. It has been said that the importance and influence of *Mein Kampf* should not be over-estimated, since the book, though widely distributed, was rarely read. That may be true; but from this observation one could draw a conclusion which may, at first sight, seem paradoxical: the book did not have to be read to become a success. The consciousness and outlook of most Germans were reflected in Hitler's book. Its contents, propagated in thousands of pamphlets, newspapers and journals, reflected the *Spießer's* heart and soul: abysmal vulgarity, overworked verbal blancmange, resentments couched in oblique metaphors, endless tirades, rhetorically painted platitudes and shallow, 'arty' dilettantism. *Mein Kampf* thus appears as the *Spießer's* mirror *par excellence*. Hitler possessed the genius of mediocrity. His 'averageness' was above average; and so it was his mediocrity that became the destiny of a nation, a nation that permitted itself to be led, step by step, away from the theory and practice of humanity.

III.

One might have expected that the complete breakdown of the German Reich would have led to a radical re-evaluation of the heritage of the past. There were indeed clear indicators of such discontinuity. Günter Eich, writing with directness, describing the situation in a lyrically reductionist, unadorned and bold style, saw an unbridgeable gulf separating the traditional idealism from the degrading historical reality. The ground had been cut away from under the cultural tradition and heritage.

Latrine

Above the stinking hole,
paper smeared with blood and urine,
swarming with buzzing flies,
I squat down low.

With an eye on wooded shores,
gardens, a stranded boat.
The hardening excrements
splash into the decaying slime.

Insane with Hölderlin's verse
resounding in my ears.
Clouds reflect their snow-white purity
in the urine.

'But go and greet the
beautiful Garonne –'
The clouds swim away
from beneath the hobbling feet.'[2]

Starting in 1945, a group of German authors turned against traditional continuity, provoking a critical discussion about traditional language and values. When the *Gruppe 47* (Group 47) first met, Günter Eich being one of the participants, Hans Werner Richter, former editor of the prohibited periodical *Der Ruf* and initiator of the group-meeting, reported:

We are listening, strenuously, concentratedly, rarely expressing our affirmation or displeasure through nods, laughter or other gestures. No one interrupts with shouts or remarks. The reader always takes his or her seat beside me. It is self-evident, it just happened. After the first reading by Wolfdietrich Schnurre, I asked, 'Well, please, some criticism. What do you have to say to it?' And suddenly something begins to happen in a form that nobody expected. The tone of the critical utterances is coarse, the sentences short, tight and unequivocal. Nobody minces matters. Every word read is weighed as to whether it is usable or outdated and used up through the years of dictatorship, the time of the great wear and tear of our language. Every sentence is examined, every unnecessary frill reproved. Big words that have lost their meaning and content are discarded, such as heart, pain, desire and sorrow [*Herz, Schmerz, Lust, Leid*]. What endures to the ears of the participants are the tight descriptive sentences. Gertrude Stein and Ernest Hemingway are in a way present in the room without anybody noticing. Dialogue and the spoken style predominate. 'Yes,' says he, or also 'no', and the 'no' and the 'yes' endure. Yet, already the next word composition 'Yes, my dear' is scornfully discarded. Who, after all, still uses 'my dear', and if he does so, he uses it in speech, but is unable to put it in writing. If he in fact does write it, it would be in an ironic sense. But irony is missing in the first years of the new beginning.[3]

A few months later, in *Tausend Gramm*, a volume of short stories by new storytellers, Wolfgang Weyrauch named the literature which had become visible *Kahlschlagliteratur* (site-levelling literature).[4] The artistic language cultivated by the bourgeoisie, the stylized 'penmanship' in all its variations, was now taboo. The bourgeois artistic language was taboo. It appeared outmoded, rusty and untruthful. 'There was nothing that endured in light of the reality in which we lived. There was a need for a new language that would make this reality transparent, a language of direct expression, clear, unequivocal and precise.'

IV.

The cultural mainstream, however, was one of confluence between continuity and discontinuity. Ambiguity, for example, characterized the observations and memories of the influential historian, Friedrich Meinecke. From a historical point of view Meinecke depicted in 1946 *Die Deutsche Katastrophe* (The German Catastrophe) without any illusions, painting German history grey on grey, with an exposition of all its mistaken paths and dead ends.[5] Yet culturally, Meinecke professed his faith in an 'internal' Germany which turned out to be an 'eternal' Germany. Meinecke concluded his monumental work by painting a 'wishful image conceived in the terrible weeks after the collapse'. This passage of the book makes clear how little the 'zero hour' actually lived up to its name.

Among the good experiences we can use, there are even some that come from the 'Third Reich'. Clever Mr. Goebbels actually knew quite well how to catch harmless souls by placing worthwhile articles in the Party's shop windows. Every Sunday morning, to distract from the church services, a 'little German treasure box' was offered on the radio. Listeners were provided with the most beautiful German music and exquisite poetic pieces. At that time I heard how old Friedrich Kayssler, shortly before the collapse, held a Goethe afternoon in the Harnack home in Dahlem, reciting Goethe's poetry in front of a small and unusually receptive audience. My thoughts turned ultimately to the Greeks, and I realized that Homer had been infused into their hearts much more through the rhapsodists than through reading [. . .]

In every German city and larger village, we hope, in the future, to establish a society of similarly inclined cultural friends, which I would like to call 'Goethe Societies' [. . .]

The 'Goethe Societies' would have the task of carrying the most lively testimonies of the great German spirit, through recitation, into the hearts of the listeners. The noblest German music and poetry would be offered at the same time[. . .] Perhaps weekly we can have a late Sunday afternoon hour, and, wherever possible, even in a church! For the religious dimension underlying our great poetry justifies, yes even demands, that it be made concrete through such symbolism. The beginning and end of such celebrations should then always be elevated through great German music, through Bach, Mozart, Beethoven, Schubert, Brahms etc.

Lyric poetry and reflective pieces should constitute the inner core of these celebrations. Those wonderful lyrics that reached their heights with Goethe and Mörike, where soul becomes nature and nature becomes soul, and those profound reflections in the style of Goethe and Schiller are perhaps 'the most German of the German' in the whole of our literature. Whoever immerses him- or herself entirely in these works, will experience, amidst all the misfortunes and the destruction of our fatherland, something indestructible, a German *character indelebilis*.

Wherever you look upon the German cultural landscape of the year 1945, you will find again and again that strange mixture of historic depression and cultural optimism. An outstanding representative of exiled German literature gave, so to speak, the motto for the new spiritual beginning leading out of the catastrophe. Thomas Mann, then living in exile in the USA, relayed over the BBC to his German listeners on 10 May 1945, two days after unconditional surrender, the message that despite the profound humiliation, this

great hour could signify Germany's return to humanity. This hour may be difficult and painful, for Germany could not bring it about on its own. Monstrous and inexplicable damage has been done to the German name, and that Germany has gambled away its power. But power isn't everything. It isn't even the main thing, and Germany's value has never come simply from its power. There was once, and there may come again, a time, when to be German meant to be esteemed for the ability to relate power to dignity through the humane contribution of the freedom of spirit.

V.

Music probably had the highest rank among Germany's preferences in 1945; it was especially well regarded as a means of survival. The importance of classical music for these times is evident much more clearly from photographs than from any statistical data. They show audiences of women and men listening, for example, to Beethoven's *Ninth Symphony*. Their faces reflect rapture, devotion to another world that illuminates their misery. It was contemplation of art without affectation, submersion without internal coquetry, celebration without pathos. It was music as a means to live, to survive. Music, Ernst Bloch informs us, because of its immediate power of human expression, possesses more than any other art form the ability to absorb the numerous sorrows, desires, and bright moments of the oppressed classes. And at this time practically everyone felt oppressed. Bloch's 'principle of hope' was also clearly present in quite another genre of music, although only for a smaller, but nevertheless substantial part of the population. Representing a break with traditional musical culture, this music did not come down from above, from the heaven of geniuses, but instead rose up anonymously from the people, who instead of using the accompaniment of classical instruments, improvised with 'dirty tones'. For this reason, and also because it was not transcendent-German, but socially immanent-American, the response to it was limited. Jazz, which during the Third Reich was an expression of inner opposition, and an aspect of some young people's resistance to the Hitler Youth, found a home in the taverns of the rubble years. Because it stood outside the European tradition, it was not recognized in established or upcoming cultural life. Particularly fatal for its future was its prohibition in schools. What was missed therefore was the possibility of inspiring young people with music, of making accessible to them an art form that meaningfully carried the feeling of and for freedom, and that evoked an unconventional creativity beyond current cultural forms.

There developed during the rubble years an 'underground' of alternative music culture, led by jazz fans. It existed in numerous variations, noted Joachim-Ernst Berendt, then an editor for Southwest Radio, who was among the first in Germany to be competently and courageously engaged with jazz. There were young men and women who, with the rhythm of jazz music, literally broke out of themselves in an enthusiasm that for middle-class citizens bore all the signs of shocking and repellent behaviour. The questions posed by Berendt provide an indirect mirror of the prevailing prejudices of the time. What creates this enthusiasm? What fascinates them about jazz? Are they unstable people who react to every momentary fad with seismographic sensitivity? Are they immature young people who lack the feelings defined by the word 'proportion'? Are they poorly brought up people lacking those human values that distinguish the Western world?

Quite a number, especially of young men, often repatriated prisoners of war coming from the USA, knew the answer: swinging melodies encouraged the lost, but surviving and recovering, generation in their difficult search for the new man, including the search for a democratic, free life. Their slogan was: 'Don't fence me in!' When Jimmy Jungermann produced one of Europe's hottest jazz programmes for Radio Munich, one-third of the 60,000 requests he received in a two-year period were for 'Don't Fence Me In'.

VI.

The resurgence of the theatre may also be characterized by the oscillation between continuity and discontinuity. Modern development was made possible by the Zurich playhouse which had been the only free German-speaking theatre in Europe during the Third Reich, with many German actors, actresses and stage-directors finding refuge there. On the day the capitulation took effect, 9 May 1945, Wolfgang Langhoff, who later in the year became director of the playhouse in Dusseldorf and then director in East Berlin, organized an 'assistance action for Germany'. Zurich actors copied plays by Giraudoux, Jean-Paul Sartre, Friedrich Wolf, Thornton Wilder, and Ferdinand Bruckner and sent them to their German colleagues. The playhouse became an information bureau. Food and clothing, as well as props, material for the curtains, and texts were collected. Above all, the Zurich Playhouse was an intellectual crossroads of great significance. Already by 6 May, Leonard Steckel, theatre chairman and stage manager, had made 'notes for the rebuilding of the theatre in free Germany [. . .]. In all probability, Germany will have no permanent theatres in the beginning of the postwar period. Guest troupes, partly organized and sent out by the occupying forces, will perform in the villages on improvised stages.' Steckel hoped that the administrators and censors of the occupying forces would recognize that theatre could be an 'important voice for democratic ideas of government. Then it would not be long before curtains would rise somewhere in the midst of the rubble of the German cities, and a festival performance would inaugurate a new, liberal theatrical season.' It was of enormous significance for such a 'liberal theatrical season' that Zurich offered a comprehensive selection of contemporary drama. Among the plays performed were: Camus's *The Just* (1950); Claudel's *The Satin Slipper* (1944); Eliot's *Family Reunion* (1945) and *Murder in the Cathedral* (1947); Giraudoux's *Undine* (1940), *Sodom and Gomorrah* (1944), and *The Madwoman of Chaillot* (1946); Garcia Lorca's *Blood Wedding* (1944); Arthur Miller's *Death of a Salesman* (1950); O'Neill's *Mourning becomes Electra* (1943) and *The Iceman Cometh* (1948); Sartre's *The Flies* and *Dirty Hands* (1948); Wilder's *Our Town* (1939); and Tennessee Williams's *The Glass Menagerie* (1947) and *A Streetcar Named Desire* (1949).

Also performed in Zurich were the works of a number of authors banned in Germany, such as Kaiser, Bruckner, Wolf, Brecht, Werfel, Hasenclever, Bruno Frank and Horvath. Highly important for Swiss drama were the contacts made between Max Frisch, Friedrich Dürrenmatt, and the epic theatre of Brecht, as well as the parable style of Thornton Wilder and John Steinbeck. Another line of development was drawn from Zurich to Brecht's Berliner Ensemble, and to the German Theatre in East Berlin. In 1947, Brecht came from Paris, visited his schoolmate Caspar Neher, and became acquainted with Oskar Wälterlin. He began to demonstrate the experimental theatre's 'aesthetic position, or at least outline an aesthetics for this theatre'. The result was the *Kleine Organon für das Theater*, a summary of his theory.[6] On 5 June 1948, his *Mr Puntila and His Servant Matti* was staged for the first time. Although Brecht directed the play, his name was not allowed to appear on the programme because of the immigration office, and thus Kurt Hirschfeld was listed as director.

Hirschfeld encouraged Max Frisch to write for theatre. The

'attempt at a requiem', *Nun singen sie wieder* ('Now They Are Singing Again'), was performed at Easter 1945, and the romance, *Santa Cruz*, in 1946. In the same year, after a trip through a devastated Germany, *Die chinesische Mauer* (The Chinese Wall) appeared as a warning in the face of collectivist suicide: 'The Flood is not irreparable'. This was followed three years later by *Als der Krieg zu Ende war* ('When the War Was Over'). Dürrenmatt's Anabaptist play, *Es steht geschrieben* ('It is Written'), was presented under the direction of Kurt Horwitz in 1947.

The authors and works which the Zürich Playhouse made accessible, mostly in German-language premières, before and after 1945, found their way into Germany relatively quickly. Leonard Steckel's prognosis that there would be no permanent theatre in Germany immediately following the war did not prove true. Instead, the curtains went up rather quickly amidst the rubble of the German cities. Thus it was very important that the walls of the self-inflicted ghetto into which the world of theatre had entered during the Third Reich were breached on the stage.

The German theatre also took advantage of theatrical competition among the Allies, whose main concern was quickly to import German translations of plays written in their own languages. The official dramatic canon of the United States comprised 60 translated works, of which about 45 were actually brought to the stage. The list of translated French plays contained 98 pieces, and that of the British, 15, all of them contemporary works. The Reichsmark was not exchangeable, and was thus practically worthless outside Germany. Therefore the military governments acquired the translation and performance rights for a specific time-period, and served as agents for the distribution of theatrical works. They valued the theatre 'especially as an instrument of cultural propaganda and re-education. Moreover, they did not want the reputation of being hostile to culture. Third, they soon broke into competition with each other. They wanted to impress each other, especially the Western Allies *vis-à-vis* the Soviets, and vice versa. Before long, the conquerors wanted to impress the conquered as well, for they needed an infantry in the war between the systems. They were therefore quick to offer bread and entertainment, especially in Berlin and Vienna, the two major cities with sectors governed by the four occupying forces.' By the way: in the Russian occupation zone intensive cultural activities were also meant to compensate for the atrocities, especially the ten thousand acts of rape which had taken place when the Russian troops entered Berlin. Now they acted with great sensitivity. Thornton Wilder's drama, *Our Little Town*, staged in East Berlin, was prohibited because the responsible Russian theatre officer thought that the Germans in their bad situation could not stand the last act, which was situated in a graveyard.

Continuity within the theatre was due to the fact that many of the actors and actresses, conductors, theatre directors and stage directors had worked under the Nazis, although in the beginning of the occupation period they had been put on blacklists. Gustav Gründgens, for example, had been manager of the Berlin *National Theater* in the Third Reich. He also received the title of privy councillor from the National Socialists, and was arrested several times after 1945. In a 1946 essay on the *Sociology of the German Actor*, he wrote that the actor was in general uninterested in politics.

> The most important thing for the actor is art or, better yet, the good role, the interesting dramatic challenge. The German actor shares this defect in political education with the entire German people [. . .] National Socialism, which was an external teaching that only worked with mass psychosis, did not really penetrate the depths, at least not consciously for most people. And so foreign observers get the astonishing picture that actors who have performed in the past 12 years have never felt themselves affected by National Socialism, and never identified themselves with their disgraceful activities. These actors, as a result, do indeed acknowledge German collective guilt.

One could assume, countered a weekly bulletin of the US military government at the end of January 1946, that no artist of note had been forced to become a member of the Nazi party. The Ministry of Propaganda handled them with kid gloves. Theatre people had to pay lip-service to National Socialism either because of their careers or because they were vulnerable to accusations of having Jewish ancestry or engaging in communist activities. Many, however, whose papers were in order, had distinguished themselves as Nazis.

Such ambivalence with respect to the activities of artists in the Third Reich led to correspondingly ambivalent reactions on the part of the Allied forces. In a 1943 study of the leading personalities of German cultural life, researched on behalf of the US government, Carl Zuckmayer wrote that actors enjoyed the Third Reich as a theatre production in which they played some role. This assertion did not, however, conform to the moral requirements with which life was to be reordered, that is, purified of National Socialism. Quasi-anecdotal events, however, documented the uncertainty of the Allies concerning this 'pretending'. Gründgens, said Zuckmayer, should in no way be considered an inscrutable villain, but as an actor-type, one who engages in the *grand jeu* both on stage as well as in real life. Gustav Gründgens and others were clever enough to overcome their affiliation with Nazi cultural policy very quickly, becoming outstanding figures in German post-war theatre.

The average productions in German theatres, however, displayed continuity. When Berthold Viertel, author, director, translator and friend of Bertolt Brecht, came to Germany, he was amazed to discover that the shallow pathos of conservative classical performances continued to have its effect. He called this old–new style *Reichskanzleistil* (Imperial Chancellery Style), having observed it on the stages of Berlin, Dusseldorf, and Vienna. 'A rare mixture has crystallized and obviously became established here, a rootless ecstasy or a cold, boastful rhetoric, which emphasized and overemphasized the official and representative parts of the production, and then changed abruptly with an all too delicate discretion that escaped into the quiet, the private and subprivate. Mania and depression followed each other without clear transitions or breaks.' The frenzied tone of violent rhetoric, the strained voice that was meant to persuade, this paroxysm that brought foam to the actor's lips, was in any case quite effective in exciting the admiration of the public, who 'regularly acknowledged the explosive tirades with enthusiastic applause'. Such observations could characterize the overall relation to classical literature during the rubble years. On the one hand, the total collapse had sensitized people to its 'beauty, truth and goodness' beyond affirmative culture and the representative pathos of 'our classicists'. On the other hand, there were no radical attempts to wrestle with, or to 'get to the roots' of the inheritance of the times.

Many of the people in the arts, as well as journalists, reporters and those who worked in broadcasting and film production, had tried to disengage or to find a niche for unpolitical activities at least during the last period of National Socialism. They found jobs rather easily in the new media-system which was established by the Allies. The step from continuity to discontinuity was often a quick step but proved to be durable, laying the foundations for a stable democratic information and communication system. Josef Müller-Marein provided an autobiographical report of such a change. In Lübeck, one day before the English arrived, he found shelter in the town theatre. He took off his military uniform and searched for something funny, something peaceful in the wardrobe. He found beige trousers, light brown jacket, both elegantly tailored, with very impressive buttons. Under the collar was sewn a note wrapped in cellophane, *Wedding Night in Paradise. Buffo Walter Müller.*

Thus I stepped out that morning, and I saw what the English would have done to me had I not managed to switch costume. They herded my comrades together. 'Quickly, quickly!' They pushed them, kicked them with their boots, fenced them in for the night in parks or on some patch of grass, and the next day ordered them to begin, without provisions, the long march to Schleswig-Holstein. I was still wearing the 'Wedding Night' outfit when we founded *Die Zeit*. I had no other civilian clothing and continued to wear it for years. When it finally fell apart and I threw it out, Marion Dönhoff said I never should have done so.

VII.

The cultural development of the Russian occupation zone in 1945 was similar to that in the Western zones, although there were the first signs of rigid repression. On the other hand, especially in Berlin, the Russian cultural officers were highly educated and had a deep knowledge of German literature, theatre, music, and philosophy. On 14 May 1945, representatives of the cultural life of Berlin met by order of the Russian military commander to discuss the resurgence of cultural life in the heavily damaged city. Already in May, many cultural events took place. On 6 June a committee of cultural personalities was put into action; the actor Paul Wegener, 70 years old, became president; secretary was Wolfgang Harich, then 24 years old. He functioned as a link to the Soviets. The poet Johannes R. Becher, who had returned to Berlin from Russian exile, founded the *Kulturbund zur demokratischen Erneuerung Deutschlands*, a league for the cultural reconstruction of Germany, finding highly placed support in East and West Germany. Antifascism should bind together all those who were willing to create a new Germany. At the first public meeting the Berlin Philharmonic Orchestra played Beethoven's *Egmont* overture. The declaration of principles concentrated upon the 'great German culture' which had been and would be the pride of the fatherland. The *Kulturbund* raised enthusiasm among many culturally minded Germans; especially since it propagated cultural continuity. As the most recent research has shown, the Soviets regarded the association as a good strategic device to strengthen and to enlarge their influence in Germany.

VIII.

Cultural beginnings in 1945, continuity and discontinuity. Only some hints could be given, some contours could be outlined. In 1995, we trace back the path of the cultural history of the Federal Republic to 1945, since *Zukunft braucht Herkunft* (the future needs roots).

I think that the recalling and visualizing of the cultural beginnings and their difficulties in 1945 is not only a matter of historical interest but of existential, vital significance for Germany. The 50th anniversary of the end of National Socialism coincides with the appearance of new right-wing and neo-nationalistic tendencies. It is therefore very important to emphasize the fact that the German individual, social and political democratic identity began on 8 May 1945, the day of unconditional surrender. With heavy losses, the Allies had finally defeated the Third Reich, giving the Germans the chance to return to humanity. The 8th of May, as the first president of the German Federal Republic, Theodor Heuß, said, is a tragic and paradoxical date – the Germans were both ruined and redeemed. The hope for a humane existence rose out of physical and spiritual debris; remembering is part of the generating of solidarity we need. In a fictional letter to his sons Heinrich Böll wrote: 'You will recognize the German mentality by the way they describe the 8th of May: as a day of defeat or of liberation.'

In his book *Über Deutschland* (About Germany) Richard Matthias Müller presents a fictional talk between father and son.

Son: In a letter to the *Frankfurter Allgemeine Zeitung* a reader proposed to celebrate the 8th of May as a national holiday.

Father: This is the day we were freed from National Socialism. A reasonable idea.

Son: You did not understand: it is the day of the unconditional surrender.

Father: I understand well. It is the day of the unconditional surrender.

Son: We should celebrate our own capitulation?
Father: We need not do it.
Son: I think we should leave it.
Father: I feel bemused.
Son: What makes you feel bemused?
Father: That you won't celebrate the end of something bad and
            the beginning of something good.[7]

The decisive sentence in this dialogue is said by the father. We must, however, hope that young people are not only willing to celebrate the 8th of May as a day of liberation but will work intensively for the aim that something like National Socialism, like Auschwitz, will never come again. The strength we need for steady democratic engagement may also come from the historical recollection of the year 1945. 'The Future needs the Past.' In those days of an almost hopeless situation the anticipatory prudence of the Western Allies and the German determination to survive laid the foundations of a state and society about which we can really be happy and modestly proud after fifty years – *So viel Anfang war nie!* (That much beginning never happened in German history). But within these fifty years on many occasions one might have thought that the bad past had not been overcome. This fatal past has again reached Germany and not only Germany in recent years: hatred against foreigners is manifest and neo-nationalistic riots take place. I do not mean that the now changed saying *Viel Anfang war nie!* (Much beginning never happened in German history) is able to characterize the actual situation of the German Federal Republic; this would be a much too negative judgement about the positive developments over decades; but it should be *a warning sign* – written on the wall to keep the democratic Germans watchful. He who goes to sleep in a democracy will awake under a dictatorship. It should be a warning sign to prevent regression into mystic mythological irrationalism again. The 'project of enlightenment' is still unfinished. To work on it is 'heavy labour'. Hans Magnus Enzensberger described the trials and tribulations of a life committed to civility and 'constitutional patriotism' in his poem of the same title – dedicated to Theodor W. Adorno:

> . . .impatiently
> despair
> in the name of the satisfied

patiently
question the despair
in the name of the despairing
impatiently patient
teach
in the name of the unteachable.[8]

Notes

1. In: *Die Sammlung*, Heft 4, 1946, p. 197 *passim*.
2. Hermann Glaser, *The Rubble Years. The Cultural Roots of Postwar Germany 1945–1948*, New York 1986, p. 6.
3. Hans Werner Richter, 'Wie entstand und was war die Gruppe 47?', in Hans A. Neunzig (ed.), *Hans Werner Richter und die Gruppe 47*, Frankfurt am Main – Berlin – Vienna 1981, p. 52 *passim* (translation H. Glaser).
4. Wolfgang Weyrauch, *Tausend Gramm*, Hamburg 1949.
5. Friedrich Meinecke, *Die Deutsche Katastrophe*, Berlin 1946.
6. Bertolt Brecht, 'Kleine Organon für das Theater', in *Sinn und Form. Sonderheft Bertolt Brecht*, ed. Johannes R. Becher *et al.*, Berlin 1949.
7. Richard Matthias Müller, *Über Deutschland*, Olten – Freiburg i. Br. 1965.
8. Hans Magnus Enzensberger, 'schwierige arbeit', in *Blindenschrift*, Frankfurt am Main 1964, p. 58 *passim* (translation H. Glaser).

ERNST VOLLRATH

Perspectives of Political Thought in Germany after 1945

I think I should begin by outlining the limitations of my chapter. They are threefold. First, I will confine my observations to academic political thought. I think I am entitled to this restriction because of the traditionally high importance attached to universities in German political culture. It may be said without much exaggeration that the bulk of political thought in Germany has been the stuff of and for university professors – and, of course, for their students.

Secondly, I will not take into consideration all university disciplines that are relevant in this respect. I have to leave out two disciplines traditionally concerned with politics, or, as I would prefer to say, with the political: historiography and, in particular, German *Allgemeine Staatslehre*. However, let me make some remarks about *Allgemeine Staatslehre* (literally: General State Teaching).

Allgemeine Staatslehre, be it a special discipline or be it incorporated into *Deutsches Staatsrecht*, should not be taken to be the equivalent of 'Constitutional Law' in Great Britain or the USA, nor of the French 'Droit Constitutionel'. We are here dealing with a peculiarity of German political culture.

The beginning of that peculiarity can be traced back to early modern times, but it has been most important in the nineteenth and twentieth centuries.[1] During that period it may well be said that *Allgemeine Staatslehre* expressed the normative political thought in Germany.

At its centre stood – and still stands – the notion of the state. But this notion of the state in German political thought exhibits two characteristic features. First: it is not the actual existing particular state, but the state as such. And secondly: this notion of the state is identified with the political. I will simply give one instance of this identificatory conception, a quotation stemming from one of the foremost German *Staatsrechtslehrer*, namely Georg Jellinek. In his *Allgemeine Staatslehre* (1900), still regarded today as a classical work, he wrote: '*Politisch* heißt *staatlich*. Im Begriff des Politischen hat man bereits den Begriff des Staates gedacht.'[2] I think it almost impossible to translate this sentence into English! (One rough translation might be: '"Political" means "of the state". By creating the concept of the Political one has already thought of the concept of the state.')

It would be most interesting to inquire whether or not this identification of the state with the political has survived. But certainly the underlying notion of the state is still present in the more conservative strand of German *Staatsrecht* today.[3] At this point I do not have space enough to present completely this German peculiarity of *Allgemeines Staatsrecht* and its implications for German political thought.

A short word may be added as to the part historiography has played in post-war German political thought. I think it is fair to say that German historiography has extensively as well as intensively explored Germany's past, particularly during the Nazi period. In this respect, German historiography may be called a truly political discipline!

Now the third limitation of my chapter. I shall not describe political thought as it was in the now extinct German Democratic Republic – and this for the simple reason that such a thing did not exist as long as the GDR existed. Everybody had to adhere to rigorously orthodox Marxism-Leninism in its Soviet interpretation, and if this can be called political thought at all, there was no room for innovative thinking. This Marxism-Leninism was imagined to be a philosophy, and the consequences have been that Philosophy, its institutions and its personnel were rigorously watched and controlled by the authorities, and everybody who tried to deviate or was simply suspected of deviation was punished immediately.[4]

To sum up it might be said that in my chapter I adhere to a statement made by George Catlin some years ago: 'Politics, like Gaul, is divided into three parts. From the "practice" of politics, at least in theory, we distinguish the "theory". But the theory itself is divided into "political science" and "political philosophy".'[5] I shall, therefore, limit myself more or less to political philosophy or normative political thinking. But to do so it will be necessary to comment also on the status of political science in Germany.

I. The Starting-point

After the complete collapse of the Nazi regime three options were open for a renewal of political thought in Germany. The precondition for any such renewal, certainly, was a complete break with Nazi ideology. Before I come to these three options two things have to be said.

First: it may be doubted that there existed any authentic political thought in Nazi ideology. Totalitarian movements and their ideologies can be understood, among other things, to be the anti-political – a revolt against any kind of ordinary politics. Nevertheless, certain elements can be identified in Nazi ideology that had an enormous impact on the practice of totalitarian politics. Although nothing in these ideological elements is authentic – what can, with revulsion, be called 'authentic' is the outrageous radicalism exhibited in the practice of realizing National Socialist political aims, and all these elements were sucked up from the cultural environment, particularly its vulgar elements[6] – there are two closely interconnected 'ideas' – a distasteful vocabulary in this context! – that can be identified in Hitler's mind:[7] the 'idea' of racially pure Nordic Man, based on vicious anti-Semitism, and the 'idea' of imperialistic expansion. The connection between these ideas is that only Nordic Man is destined to dominate the *Lebensraum* (conquered spaces) and exterminate the indigenous population or subjugate and exploit it.

Secondly: it is sadly true that quite a number of the old élite tried to adjust to the new regime and to Nazi ideology, and this even holds true for the academic world. In order to understand, not to justify, this adjustment, it may be said that it originated in the traditionally apolitical centre of German culture and formal cultural self-perception.[8] One of the problems with this cultural self-perception is that between the true cultural elements and the vulgar elements there existed no sharp distinction, so that the one could be taken for the other.

Among these members of the German academic world I want to mention only German two *Staatsrechtslehrer*,[9] these being the most

famous: Carl Schmitt and Martin Heidegger.[10] One should keep in
mind what Hannah Arendt said, namely that all these men – she
mentioned Carl Schmitt, but certainly thought of Martin Heidegger
as well – never had any real influence *after* the stabilization of the
regime.[11] They were used and misused to muster the support of the
population and to clothe the regime with a pretence of respectability.
Some of these people – very few – were removed from their academic
positions after the war, although not without a good pension, as in
the case of the above-mentioned Carl Schmitt. The others adjusted
cheerfully to the new situation. To use an expression coined with
regard to the situation after the breakdown of 'real existing
socialism' in the GDR: they became *Wendehälse* ('wrynecks' or
turncoats).

I finally come to the three options that were open to German political thought after the collapse of the Nazi regime. These three
options were:

1. to return to those traditions of German political thought that
   had not been spoiled or ruined by contact with Nazi ideology;
2. to adopt the political thinking of Western political culture; and
3. to profit from the experience of the emigrants who had had to
   flee to Western countries, some of whom now returned.

All of these options were taken up, either separately or, in most
cases, conjointly. The conjunction seemed to be obvious. Going back
to an unspoiled tradition of German political thought included a
universalistic approach to principles and values shared throughout
Occidental culture. And the emigrants and re-immigrants had
acquainted themselves with exactly these principles and values as
they were to be found in the institutions of Western political culture
and in their intellectual foundations.

On the initiative of the American military government in
Germany the ministers of culture and of justice of the *Land* of
Hessen invited their colleagues of the other *Länder* in the three
Western zones to attend a conference that took place from 10 to 11
September 1949, in the *Jagdschloß* (hunting lodge) *Waldleiningen*.[12] The
conference can be taken as the starting-point of a restructuring
designed to create institutes of political science at almost all
German universities. Originally the idea behind these foundations
had been not so much a scientific or theoretical one, but a pedagogic
or an educational one, as political science was explicitly supposed to

be a science of *Demokratiewissenschaft* – the study of democracy. They developed into institutions of teaching and of research, as did all the other institutes of political science in the Western world.[13]

From its very beginning and for a long time thereafter the whole discipline took American Political Science as its paradigm, and followed this paradigm obediently in all its theoretical and methodological orientations. This linkage of German political science to American political science goes as far as to exclude virtually all other orientations, particularly French political theory (not French philosophy!). Even such an eminent figure as Michael Oakeshott is almost completely absent in German intellectual life. Only one of his books was translated into German, without much success.[14] And it turned out that it was quite impossible to translate his magisterial work 'On Human Conduct'.

II. An Attempt to Organize the Field

What I want to do in this section is to show the interaction of two tendencies in German political thought after 1945. One might speak of their intermarriage. The first tendency has always been the attempt to win access to the universal – at least universally Western – way of thinking; and the second tendency was the preservation, sometimes almost unconsciously, of certain peculiarities of traditional German thinking.

It has become customary to differentiate between three theoretical and methodological approaches in the field of political science and political theory, at least in so far as these disciplines are taught in German universities and in the institutes of political science and of philosophy.[15] Numerous introductions to the subject have made use of the differentiation,[16] and, although the usefulness of the differentiation has been questioned, I will employ it here.[17]

The three approaches are:

1. the analytic–empirical approach,
2. the dialectic–critical approach, and
3. the normative–essentialistic approach.

(I shall comment on the first paradigm, which sometimes claims to be the only scientific one, and then turn to the two other paradigms.)

1. *Mainstream Political Science in Germany*

The analytic–empirical paradigm of political science aspires to fulfil the standards of rigorous science using the paraphernalia of social science proper: quantitative research technologies and analytic mathematical methodologies. Its most widespread application is to the investigation of voters' behaviour and research into public choices. The model has been, and still is, American Political Science. Its programme can be formulated, in the words of David Easton, as one of transforming political science 'into a science modelled after the methodological assumptions of natural science'.[18] One may quote Alfred Cobban's ironical remark: 'What is called political science [. . .] seems to me a device, invented by university teachers, for avoiding that dangerous subject, politics, without achieving science.'[19] Be that as it may, after the Second World War American Political Science has universally served in the Western hemisphere as the model for a political theory that claimed to be scientific. The situation in Germany was not different from that in many other countries, and in its institutes of political science all the orientations and almost all the changing fashions of American Political Science have been adopted and/or imitated. Together with this brand of analytic empiricism – empiricism using the methodological tools of analytical social research technologies – the mainstream of political science at German universities used another kind of empiricism that I would like to call descriptive empiricism, an empiricism describing the modes of government in different countries or the foreign policies of the different powers, etc.

I shall now give an example to show how German political science took over a new orientation from American Political Science. I refer to the paradigm of political culture. It may well be that the term 'political culture' was actually coined by a German: Johann Gottfried Herder.[20] But for its use as a concept of modern political science it has to be said – to use biblical language: in the beginning were Almond and Verba.

In 1956 Gabriel A. Almond submitted a paper, 'Comparative Political Systems', to the 'Committee on Comparative Politics' of the Social Science Research Council of Princeton University.[21] In this paper he wrote: 'Every political system is embedded in a particular pattern of orientation to political action. I have found it useful to refer to this as a political culture.'[22] The term, as a concept of political science, was coined, and a new research programme was originated that led straight to a new branch of political science. The basic methodological orientations were analytic and descriptive, the theoretical claim was comparative. The standards, according to which the political cultures of different societies were assessed and judged, were taken, without much reflection, from paradigmatic American – and to a lesser degree English-examples.

The first to introduce the term 'political culture' as a concept of and for political science into German usage seems to have been Ekkehard Krippendorf in a review-article first published in 1965.[23] From then on the concept, and with it the research programme, entered German political science and expanded rapidly. The full corpus of this literature, which began to be produced within a couple of years, can hardly be mastered any more.[24]

However, there exists a characteristic difference between the American and the German treatment of the concept and programme of 'political culture'. Whereas in American political science the descriptive–analytical, almost neutral, use of both the term and the programme, prevails, in Germany both have acquired a highly critical colour. They are often taken to indicate the deficit in or even the complete lack of political culture in today's Germany.[25] The sometimes acid critique is based upon a concept of pure democracy, the absence of which is deplored deeply and seen as contributing to Germany's disastrous traditions.

The term finally entered the everyday language of politicians and journalists. That caused a German newspaper pointedly to remark: 'Whenever these politicians talk about political culture what they have in mind is the non-culture of others.'[26]

2. Neo-Marxism in West Germany

On the basis of the tripartite differentiation of approaches in the field of political science/political theory, strange combinations are possible. The analytic–empirical and the dialectic–critical approaches go together in their claim to be 'scientific' approaches – that is, over and against normative–'essentialistic' approaches, although, of course, their respective understandings of what constitutes this scientific character are absolutely different. On the other hand, the dialectic–critical and the normative–'essentialistic' approaches share an aversion towards the positivist restrictions of empirical–analytic political science.

What has chastely been baptized 'the dialectic–critical approach' is nothing but a branch of Neo-Marxism. After the Second World War and after the partition of Germany, any orthodox Marxism of the Leninist brand such as prevailed in East Germany would have stood no chance in Western Germany. There were very few Marxists left; most of them went to East Germany, and quite a few came back after having experienced 'real existing socialism'.

The revival of non-orthodox Marxism was not brought about by the old members of the 'Critical Theory' school, returning from emigration to the USA – above all Max Horkheimer and Theodor Adorno.[27] They carefully hid their Marxist leanings – and were later heavily attacked for doing so by younger colleagues – as they had already done during the Weimar period and during their stay in the USA. The intellectual revival of unorthodox Neo-Marxism in West Germany after 1945 can almost be attributed to one single person: Jürgen Habermas. Since I intend to comment on his thinking later I shall confine myself here to some general remarks.

The Neo-Marxism of Critical Theory has always understood itself as an oppositionist school of thought, and this in a twofold sense: both theoretically and politically. Theoretically, the opposition was directed against what its supporters labelled the positivism of mainstream political science and of science as such. Although claiming to possess a superior type of theory, this opposition did not confine itself to mere theoretical discourse, but was accompanied by political argumentation. Positivist science, so it argued, being an emanation of the existing political and social system, will of necessity affirm that system and is, therefore, unable to criticize it, let alone to head the opposition necessary to have it changed. The paradigm behind this project was the idea of democracy pure and unalienated in the sense described by Rousseau. And politically, although the supporters of Critical Theory never sympathized with 'real existing socialism', the breakdown of the Soviet Union and the German Democratic Republic was experienced as a heavy blow.

3. *Political Philosophy*

One of the peculiarities of the German situation is the survival of political philosophy – there has been no Peter Laslett to exclaim that 'anyway' political philosophy is dead. In the German context, however, political philosophy has always been identified with practical, i. e. moral, philosophy, and it may well be said that an autonomous theory of the political hardly existed in Germany. It might even be better to speak about 'normative practical theory'. The situation is the more complex, since there existed two academic institutions in which this orientation could develop: institutes of political science and institutes of philosophy.

When some of the emigrants came back to Germany – either permanently or temporarily – they often had a great influence on the theoretical orientation of the newly founded institutes of political science, either as the founders of the institutions or as heads of department. They not only brought with them the knowledge of American Political Science, but a strong normative and even philosophical orientation, deriving both from traditional German education and from the encounter with the tradition of classical American political culture of the generation of the Founding Fathers. To mention two representatives: Arnold Bergstraesser at the University of Freiburg im Breisgau and Eric Voegelin at the University of Munich have founded what might be called 'schools', schools which were not quite so widely acknowledged as the 'Frankfurt school', but which nevertheless were quite influential.

There exists another set of institutions where normative political theory and political philosophy have their place: the institutes of philosophy, which means that two types of German academic institution are concerned with normative or philosophical political theory. As these two developed almost independently the one from the other, it is hardly possible to give a periodization that covers the whole spectrum. To a certain degree, two dates stand out: 1968, the year of the students' revolt, and 1989, the year of the coming down of the Berlin Wall and the collapse of the German Democratic Republic. I shall comment on 1989 later.

In 1972 and 1974, Manfred Riedel, from the University of Erlangen, put together two large volumes on normative practical theory: *Rehabilitierung der praktischen Philosophie*.[28] (By the way: why 'rehabilitation'? Because the general opinion was, that 'practical philosophy' had come to an end in Germany after the death of Hegel!) These two volumes present an almost complete overview of German political philosophy after 1945 until the date of their publication.[29] Here all the protagonists and most of the topics that appeared in their controversies are assembled, and if one were to project the essential lines of these debates up to the present time one would certainly discover that nothing essentially new has appeared in the meantime. Unfortunately the two volumes have not found a sequel. But certain continuing features of German 'political philosophy' can readily be discovered and identified.

First, as the title of Professor Riedel's publication indicates, if it is considered by name at all, political philosophy in the German context is regarded as forming part of 'practical philosophy', and 'practical philosophy' is equated with 'moral philosophy'. There is a strong tendency in German political philosophy to treat the principles and even the possibility of authentic political philosophy exclusively through the use of moral categories, moral principles – in short moral argumentation. To conceive of political philosophy, and what would amount to the same, to conceive of the principles of politics and the political in autonomous political terms – as an example in English political discourse I would quote Sir Isaiah Berlin, like Michael Oakeshott almost completely unknown in Germany – is rather rare, if not unheard of.

Secondly, another strong characteristic feature of German political theory is its broad historical orientation. Almost never is the attempt made to develop a theoretical discourse without reference to the tradition of political philosophy in the Western world from its Greek origins on. What dominates are monographs on one or another of the classics: Aristotle, Kant, Hegel, Marx – and there are some very good ones! This is not to say that other political thinkers did not receive attention from time to time. For instance: quite recently a couple of books have been written on Machiavelli,[30] and this may indicate a renewed interest in an autonomous theory of the political. And a particular historical interest has been shown in earlier political thinking of the sixteenth to the eighteenth centuries in Germany. All this may indicate a rediscovery of an older tradition of German political thought. But the four names I have just mentioned are the names of the political theorists who serve most prominently as references for today's German political thinking. The treatment of the political thinking connected with these names does not simply serve as a historical presentation, but as a systematic paradigm: one chooses either to adhere to the Aristotelian model or to the Kantian model of political thinking – or is accused of doing so! I shall return to this point later.

I would like to draw attention to yet another development in recent German political thought. In the English-speaking world there existed and still exists a type of literature that was not completely absent from German literature, but certainly lacked there that preeminence it possesses here: I mean books with titles such as: 'A History of Political Thought', and the like – and I need only mention the names of George H. Sabine, William A. Dunning or John G. Gunnell. The function of this type of literature was – and still is – to acquaint the reader, for instance college students, with an essential part of Western culture, or at least to provide them with some knowledge about politics and the political.

But quite recently several books have been published in Germany that provide comprehensive information on the history of political thought. Of these books I want to mention two. The first is a five-volume collection, edited by Iring Fetscher and Herfried Münkler, *Pipers Handbuch der politischen Ideen*.[31] The second was published by a governmental agency, the *Bundeszentrale für politische Bildung*, by Hans-Joachim Lieber (ed.), *Politische Theorien von der Antike bis zur Gegenwart*.[32] It might be added that a section of one of the German societies of political science, the *Deutsche Vereinigung für Politische Wissenschaft*, has made considerable efforts to ground *Theoriegeschichte* (not quite identical with the older 'history of political ideas') firmly as part of the discipline.[33] All this points, in my judgement, to a growing demand for information on politics and the political in Germany.

III. The Lines of Conflict

Any and every living scientific and theoretic discipline must display conflicts and controversies on many topics: it is simply a sign of liveliness! This also holds true for the disciplines concerned with politics and the political in Germany. I shall begin to comment on this by pointing to one strange exception: there is almost no relation between political science/political theory and that German peculiarity, *Allgemeines Staatsrecht*. Since, in my judgement, *Allgemeines Staatsrecht* plays an important part in the German perception of the political, this lack is the more disturbing.

There is another controversy upon which I need not comment: the controversy between political theory conceived as a science built upon the methodological assumptions of the natural sciences and a political theory that admits philosophical reflection and normative argumentation. This controversy is not peculiar to German political science, and has been fought out in the Anglo–American world as well. It is my pleasure to quote John Plamenatz, the doyen of English Political Philosophy: 'They [i. e. those who insist on the scientific

character pure and simple of any authentic political theory; E.V.] see
the nonsense in these doctrines [. . .] They are too ready to assume
that where they have seen nonsense there is no sense which they
have not seen.'[34]

There are two other controversies upon which I want to comment.
The first is theoretical, the second more political. But one should
keep in mind that in the field of political theory theoretical
controversies tend to become political conflicts. As I have said
earlier, theoretical orientations refer to classical positions. The first,
the theoretical controversy, has been carried through as a conflict
between a more Kantian position and a more Aristotelian position.
The protagonist of the Kantian position is Karl-Otto Apel, and his
basic assumption is that all and every political and practical action
and *a fortiori* each and every institution must be legitimized by
Letztbegründung (an ultimate grounding) in a consensus arrived at by
communicative argumentation. This communicative argumentation
is based upon transcendentally necessary normative principles that
must be accepted if one wishes to participate at all in rational
discourse. This is called a 'Transformation of Philosophy',[35] namely
of a philosophy of the Kantian type. Particularly some of the
followers of Apel have transformed this kind of argumentation into a
political discourse. The young Habermas adopted this concept of
communicative community, but is reducing more and more the
conditions needed to arrive at such a consensus.

The opponents of this concept have been accused of (Neo-)
Aristotelianism,[36] founding ethical norms on mere custom and
empirical consensus. Their argumentation against the idea of an *a
priori* notion of a communicative community serving as a norm for
political action and political institutions is based on the counter-
factual character of this idea and on the impossibility of arriving at
any such consensus within any finite time.[37]

The other conflict, the more political one, has been fought out even
more bitterly. Most political theorists in Germany have repeatedly
founded and grounded, defended and explained again and again,
liberal representative democracy. But from the very beginning of the
Federal Republic of Germany there have been some who have doubted
or even denied its democratic character. The method of doing so was
the construction of a fundamental contradiction between the actually
existing liberal state, and a *Rechtsstaat* (a state under the rule of law)
and the idea of pure and unalienated democracy, an idea connected
with the Rousseauian–Marxian concept of class-society and class

domination. One of the first protagonists of this kind of thinking in West Germany was the late Wolfgang Abendroth,[38] who promoted Jürgen Habermas to a lectureship since his own teacher, Max Horkheimer, refused to do so because he was afraid of furthering the career of a Marxist. Horkheimer, therefore, was later attacked by followers of Habermas for having supported the conservative tendencies of the Adenauer era!

But this line of thinking, criticizing the Federal Republic for not being a real democracy but a tyranny in disguise, was pursued by quite a number of younger people, sometimes in a rather vulgar manner.[39] The problem for this kind of argumentation was always the existence of the German Democratic Republic. If one takes away the bitterness with which this controversy was fought, what remains is the question of what the concept of democracy really means and what were the conditions of its realization. In opposition here were the concepts of pure democracy as such and of mediated democracy of the republican type. In the field of politics political controversies are often accompanied by theoretical conflicts.

Together with this conflict came another one. It had to do with the question whether or not 'totalitarianism' or 'fascism' must be regarded as offering the correct interpretative categorization for the understanding of the epochal events of our century. The front line clearly ran between 'Leftists', who, although usually they never uttered any sympathy with the reality of socialism in the Soviet Union and the other countries of the Red Empire, did not want to accept structural analogics between the two totalitarian systems, and the defenders of liberal democracy. The argument that the concept of 'totalitarianism' was nothing but an invention of the Cold War can certainly be refuted.[40] It originated in Italy in the period between the two World Wars and from its very invention on was intended to distinguish between liberal democracy on the one hand and communism/fascism on the other. In any case, the battle over these concepts has been fought out with bitterness and harshness.[41] The battle proved again that in the field of politics all theoretical controversies are political ones.

IV. Three Exemplary Representatives

I now want to present three major figures in political discourse in Germany: Carl Schmitt, Jürgen Habermas and Hannah

Arendt. All three may be called representative for one or the other of the possibilities of political thought. It should be noted, however, that in this context I cannot exhaustively interpret their complex political thought. I shall confine myself to certain features that seem to be indicative.

1. Carl Schmitt

Carl Schmitt consistently opposed the liberal constitution of the Weimar republic, and openly supported the Nazi regime after it had come to power in 1933. Shortly before that happened he had pointed to the possibility of ostracizing both extreme parties, the Communist Party and the Nazi Party. Now he offered a theory to legitimize totalitarian politics, and this considerably promoted his career. In 1936 he came under attack by the *Schwarze Corps*, a magazine of the SS, and somewhat withdrew from the public eye, but continued to lecture and to publish without any serious difficulty. In 1945 he was questioned by the prosecution at the Nuremberg Trials, but was not accused. Dismissed from his university position, he withdrew to a little place – Plettenberg – he called his 'San Casciano', thus alluding to Machiavelli's refuge.

After 1945 his political thinking – not to mention his political opinions! – first underwent sharp critique[42] and was exhaustively and critically examined.[43] In my judgement the political thinking of Carl Schmitt and his disastrous political opinions should to a large extent be understood in relation to German *Staatsrechtslehre* and the crisis into which this doctrine had run at the end of the nineteenth century, together with the elements of the politics of cultural despair (Fritz Stern) that accompanied this crisis.[44]

In 1986 and for the first time since 1945 a conference on Carl Schmitt was held at the *Hochschule für Verwaltungswissenschaft* (Speyer). In his foreword to the publication of the conference papers Helmut Quaritsch, who had organized the conference, declared: 'Carl Schmitt's support of the Nazi state has been known sufficiently to the participants of the conference', and: 'this does not justify a scientific-political *damnatio memoriae* of an author who published for 68 years, whose publications belong to the most stimulating works stemming from the pen of a German jurist in this century, and who, like no other jurist, has had an impact beyond the limits of his profession'.[45] Ever since then the number of books and essays on Carl Schmitt has increased.[46]

The complexities and the sensitivities of the treatment of Carl Schmitt were revealed when an American scholar, Ellen Kennedy, pointed to certain analogies between Carl Schmitt and Critical Theory, particularly in their treatment of liberalism. She had done so at a conference devoted to 'The Frankfurt School and its Consequences'. Her paper was excluded from the publication, and when her essay 'Carl Schmitt und die "Frankfurter Schule", Deutsche Liberalismuskritik im 20. Jahrhundert' was finally published in the journal *Geschichte und Gesellschaft*, it was accompanied by three essays written by supporters of Critical Theory, who flatly rejected her theses. What was not published was the article with which Miss Kennedy answered these massive attacks. Her rejoinder finally was published – together with the three articles of her opponents – in the American magazine *Telos*.[47] In German political discourse the name of Carl Schmitt serves as the head of Medusa, and anybody who is connected with that name is immediately ostracized.

2. Jürgen Habermas

In a review-article on several translations of works of Carl Schmitt into English, Jürgen Habermas declared: 'The really problematic move which Carl Schmitt makes is, admittedly, the separation of liberalism and democracy.'[48] This declaration, which should be seen in the light of the controversy just mentioned, seems somewhat strange because in the ever-changing orientations of Habermas's political thought he had always been firm on the separation of liberalism and democracy.

His intellectual and theoretical positions in this respect have changed considerably, though; changed to such an extent that the original position is hardly recognizable. He started as an orthodox Neo-Marxist in the sense of 'Critical Theory', using *Erkenntnistheorie* (a theory of cognition) as *Gesellschaftstheorie* (a theory of society). But in trying to uphold this programme he was finally forced to give up two of its essential elements: its concept of totality and the metaphysics of history, namely, those elements that validated his claim to be a Marxist.

He tried to mend the holes in the theory by adopting a number of other theoretical projects: the discourse ethics of Karl-Otto Apel, the hermeneutics of H.-G. Gadamer, Anglo-Saxon speech act theory, Hannah Arendt's phenomenology of acting, Popper's falsification theory, Kohlenberger's evolutionary theory of cognition, even Luhmann's functional systems theory. The product of these elements, which do not fit easily together, is the strange theory of a twofold concept of the political developed in his new book *Faktizität und Geltung*, in which he tried – unsuccessfully in my judgement[49] – to develop a coherent concept of the political that does justice to the actually existing liberal society and at the same time remains critical of its democratic deficits.

3. Hannah Arendt

I shall not even try to give a short overview of Hannah Arendt's political thought. I want to point only to one element. It has been said that her thinking is oriented to the sunken ruins of the *polis* of antiquity and is dominated by hellenizing nostalgia. I think that this is a misunderstanding. She combines the tradition of German philosophical thought – to which, indeed, an orientation to the *polis* belongs – with her American experiences. She once confessed that her paradigms were the American Revolution and the Constitution of the United States,[50] not, as has usually been asserted, the Greek *polis*, the 'sunken city'.

Hannah Arendt's political thinking did not have a major impact in Germany except on some very few people. What, if anything, has been taken up positively has been her concept of totalitarianism, putting together Stalinism and National Socialism as the two exemplary cases, and her interpretation of the Eichmann case. But she has rather been considered as a political essayist than as a serious political theorist.

V. The Winds of Change

Did the events of 1989 and after, the breakdown of the Berlin Wall, the collapse of the German Democratic Republic, the unification of Germany, and the decline of the Soviet Empire, have any impact on German political thought? Certainly they did! And I shall comment on two developments within German political thought after 1989 which in my judgement are characteristic for changes, the real outcome of which is still before us in the future.

The first change occurred with the German Left. Jürgen

Habermas, ever a beacon for those who are lost in the dark, exclaimed: 'The non-communist Left has no reason to wear sackcloth and ashes; but neither can they pretend that nothing has happened.'[51] What really happened was that the German Left switched its dominating paradigm! Now that Marx proved to be dead – at least for a while – they discovered Hannah Arendt,[52] and took up her thinking, or what they thought to be her thinking, as the new paradigm. This is the more astonishing as before the collapse of the former paradigm she had been attacked fiercely by the Left as a Cold Warrior or even as belonging to the fascist expressionists such as Ernst Jünger and Carl Schmitt. At this moment it is not quite clear what this paradigm-change really means. It may indicate a return to a more realistic picture of politics!

The second change that took place is a new discourse on the German nation. This is a rather old question, and it was first formulated by those intellectuals at the end of the eighteenth century who, themselves excluded from any active role in the field of politics, perceived a deficit, a lack of a unified state,[53] and replaced it with the notion of the specificity of German culture. After 1945 there was no longer any serious attempt to broach this ancient question for fear of being accused of Nationalism.

When unification was accomplished – all of a sudden and unexpectedly; nobody had foreseen it, nobody was prepared – it should not be a surprise that this discussion burst forth again. Whatever this discussion means, it should be noted that Germany for the first time in her history has frontiers, in the East as well as in the West, that are accepted both by her neighbours and by herself.

It is quite clear that the former Left was not too happy with German unification. The dream of an other, of a different, Germany vanished, as had so many of the dreams of the Left. But was it really necessary to comment on these events with so many acid judgements: *DM-Nationalismus?* Let it be!

Apart from these voices and apart from the voice of Günther Grass, who played the notion of *Kulturnation* (cultural-nation) against that of *Staatsnation* (state-nation), the general mood of this discussion[54] is an acceptance of the newly existing Germany and the assurance that this Germany will accept all the responsibilities connected with its status as a nation among other nations.[55]

Notes

1. A comprehensive history of all the juridical disciplines in Germany occupied with the state or centred around the state has been written by Michael Stolleis, *Geschichte des öffentlichen Rechts in Deutschland*, Erster Band: *Reichspublizistik und Policeywissenschaft 1600–1800*, Munich 1988, Zweiter Band: *Staatsrechtslehre und Verwaltungswissenschaft 1800–1914*, Munich 1992.
2. Georg Jellinek, *Allgemeine Staatslehre*, 3rd edn, Leipzig 1913, p. 180.
3. See: *Handbuch des Staatsrechts der Bundesrepublik Deutschland*, ed. Josef Isensee and P. Kirchhoff, Heidelberg 1987, Bd. 1. *Grundlagen von Staat und Verfassung*, § *13, Staat und Verfassung* (J. Isensee), Rn 1: Der Verfassungsstaat der Bundesrepublik Deutschland ist Staat, p. 592.
4. N. Kapferer, *Das Feindbild der marxistisch–leninistischen Philosophie in der DDR 1945–1988*, Darmstadt 1990.
5. G. Catlin, 'Political Theory: What is it?', *Political Science Quarterly*, Vol. LXXII (1957), p. 2.
6. See for instance: Fritz Stern, *Kulturpessimismus als politische Gefahr*, 2nd edn, Frankfurt am Main 1986 (1963); originally published as *The Politics of Cultural Despair*, San Francisco 1961.
7. Eberhard Jäckel, *Hitlers Weltanschauung*, 2nd edn, Frankfurt am Main 1983.
8. See my essay: 'Die Kultur des Politischen, Konzepte politischer Wahrnehmung in Deutschland', in Volker Gerhardt (ed.), *Der Begriff der Politik, Bedingungen und Gründe politischen Handelns*, Stuttgart 1990, p. 268 *passim*.
9. Ernst-Wolfgang Böckenförde (ed.), *Staatsrecht und Staatsrechtslehre im Dritten Reich*, Heidelberg 1985.
10. See the author's articles: 'Wie ist Carl Schmitt an seinen Begriff des Politischen gekommen?', *Zeitschrift für Politik* 36 (1989), p. 151 *passim*; 'Politik und Existenz', *Politisches Denken*, Jahrbuch 1991, Stuttgart 1992, p. 156 *passim*; 'Martin Heidegger, Die Politik und das Politische', *Göttingische Gelehrte Anzeigen* 242 (1990), p. 120 *passim*.
11. Hannah Arendt, *Elemente und Ursprünge totaler Herrschaft*, Frankfurt am Main 1953, p. 506.
12. Die politischen Wissenschaften an den deutschen Universitäten und Hochschulen, Gesamtprotokoll der Konferenz von Waldleinigen vom 10. und 11. September 1949, ed. Ministerium für Erziehung und Volksbildung, Hesse.
13. Two histories of the discipline in Germany from two opposite positions should be mentioned: H. Kastendiek, *Die Entwicklung der westdeutschen Politikwissenschaft*, Frankfurt am Main 1977; H.-J. Arndt, *Die Besiegten von 1945, Versuch einer Politologie für Deutsche samt Würdigung der Politikwissenschaft in der Bundesrepublik Deutschland*, Berlin 1978.

14.   Michael Oakeshott, *Rationalismus in der Politik*, Neuwied 1966.
15.   For a rigorous critique of this tripartite differentiation: E. Faul, 'Politikwissenschaft in Deutschland, Bemerkungen zu Entwicklungstendenzen und Entwicklungsanalysen,' *Politische Vierteljahresschrift* 20 (1979), p. 71 *passim*.
16.   To give only one example: Klaus von Beyme, *Die politischen Theorien der Gegenwart*, Munich – Zurich 1972, numerous editions!
17.   For a more elaborate discussion see my book: *Grundlegung einer philosophischen Theorie des Politischen*, Würzburg 1987, p. 167 *passim*.
18.   David Easton, *A Framework for Political Analysis*, Englewood Cliffs, NJ, 1965, p. 8. Highly critical: Bernard Crick, *The American Science of Politics, Its Origins and Conditions*, San Francisco 1959.
19.   A. Cobban, 'The Decline of Political Theory', *Political Science Quarterly* 68 (1953), p. 335.
20.   Johann Gottfried Herder, *Ideen zur Philosophie der Geschichte und der Menschheit, Gesammelte Werke* (Suphan) XIV, 87. This information is to be found in: F.M. Barnard, 'Culture and Political Development, Herder's Suggestive Insight', *The American Political Science Review* 63 (1969), p. 92, note 61.
21.   Published in *Journal of Politics* 18 (1956), pp. 391–409.
22.   Ibid.
23.   Ekkehard Krippendorf, 'Politische Wissenschaft in USA', in Ekkehard Krippendorf, *Political Science – Amerikanische Beiträge zur Politikwissenschaft*, Tübingen 1965, pp. 1–22.
24.   A certain overview can be found in: W.M. Iwand, *Paradigma Politische Kultur: Konzepte, Methoden, Ergeignisse der Political Culture-Forschung in der Bundesrepublik*, Opladen 1985; see also: D. Berg-Schlosser, Politische Kultur, *Eine neue Dimension politikwissenschaftlicher Forschung*, Munich 1972; D. Berg-Schlosser, Jakob Schissler (eds), 'Politische Kultur in Deutschland', Sonderheft 18 (1987) of *Politische Vierteljahresschrift*.
25.   For instance: Martin and Sylvia Greifenhagen, *Ein schwieriges Vaterland, Zur politischen Kultur in Deutschland*, Munich 1979; H. Brüggemann *et al.*, *Über den Mangel an politischer Kultur in Deutschland*, Berlin 1978.
26.   *Frankfurter Allgemeine Zeitung*, from 31 January 1986, Nr. 26, p. 1.
27.   The history of 'Critical Theory' or the 'Frankfurt School' has been richly documented in the following books (all written by supporters): U. Migdal, *Die Frühgeschichte des Frankfurter Instituts für Sozialforschung*, Frankfurt – New York 1981; M. Gangl, *Politische Ökonomie und Kritische Theorie, Ein Beitrag zur theoretischen Entwicklung der Frankfurter Schule*, Frankfurt – New York 1987; M. Jay, *Dialektische Phantasie, Die Geschichte der Frankfurter Schule und des Instituts für Sozialforschung 1923–1950*, Frankfurt a. Main 1985; R. Wiggershaus, *Die Frankfurter Schule; Geschichte, Theoretische Entwicklung, Politische Bedeutung*, Munich – Vienna 1986.

28. Manfred Riedel, *Rehabilitierung der praktischen Philosophie*, Bd. 1: *Geschichte – Probleme – Aufgaben*, Freiburg 1972; Bd. 2: *Rezeption, Argumentation, Diskussion*, Freiburg 1974.

29. There exists another overview: 'Franco Volpi, La rinascita della filosofia practica in Germania', in Claudio Pacchiani (ed.), *Filosofia pratica e scienza politica*, Abano Terme (Padova) 1980.

30. See my review-article: 'Neue Machiavelli-Literatur', *Zeitschrift fürHistorische Forschung* 20 (1993), p. 505 *passim*.

31. Iring Fetscher and Herfried Münkler (eds), *Pipers Handbuch der politischen Ideen*, Bd. 1: *Frühe Hochkulturen und europäische Antike*, Munich – Zurich 1988; Bd. 2: *Mittelalter: Von den Anfängen des Islam bis zur Reformation*, Munich – Zurich 1993: Bd. 3: *Neuzeit: Von den Konfessionskriegen bis zur Aufklärung*, Munich – Zurich 1985; Bd. 4: *Neuzeit: Von der Französischen Revolution bis zum europäischen Nationalismus*, Munich – Zurich 1986; Bd. 5: *Neuzeit: Vom Zeitalter des Imperialismus bis zu den neuen sozialen Bewegungen*, Munich – Zurich 1987.

32. Hans-Joachim Lieber (ed.), *Politische Theorien von der Antike bis zur Gegenwart*, Schriftenreihe der Bundeszentrale für politische Bildung, Bd. 299, Bonn 1991. To avoid misunderstandings, it should be added that the publication is suitably objective in its scientific orientation.

33. U. Bermbach (ed.), 'Politische Ideengeschichte, Probleme einer Teildisziplin der Politischen Wissenschaft', Sonderheft 15 (1984) of *Politische Vierteljahresschrift*.

34. J. Plamenatz, 'The Use of Political Theory', now in A. Quinton (ed.), *Political Philosophy*, Oxford Readings in Philosophy, Oxford University Press 1967, numerous reprints, p. 22. The allusion to Oxford as the English Rome of political philosophy is Plamenatz's own.

35. Karl-Otto Apel, *Transformation der Philosophie*, Bd. 1. *Sprachanalytik, Semiotik, Hermeneutik*; Bd. 2. *Das Apriori der Kommunikationsgemeinschaft*, Frankfurt am Main 1973.

36. Hermann Schnädelbach, 'Was ist Neoaristotelianismus?', in W. Kuhlmann (ed.), *Moralität und Sittlichkeit, Das Problem Hegels und die Diskursethik*, Frankfurt am Main 1986, p. 38 *passim*.

37. Odo Marquard, *Abschied vom Prinzipiellen, Philosophische Studien*, Stuttgart 1981; Hermann Lübbe, *Politischer Moralismus, Der Triumpf der Gesinnung über die Urteilskraft*, Berlin 1987.

38. Wolfgang Abendroth, *Antagonistische Gesellschaft und politische Demokratie*, Neuwied – Berlin 1967.

39. Reinhard Kühnl, *Formen bürgerlicher Herrschaft, Liberalismus – Faschismus*, Reinbek bei Hamburg 1971.

40. Jens Petersen, 'Die Enstehung des Totalitarismusbegriffs in Italien', in Manfred Funke (ed.), *Totalitarismus. Ein Studienreader zur Herrschaftsanalyse moderner Diktaturen*, Düsseldorf 1978, p. 105 *passim*.

41. Karl Dietrich Bracher, *Zeitgeschichtliche Kontroversen, Um Faschismus, Totalitarismus, Demokratie*, Munich 1976.

42. Christian von Krokow, *Die Entscheidung, Eine Untersuchung über Ernst Jünger, Carl Schmitt, Martin Heidegger*, Stuttgart 1958; J. Fijalkowski, *Die Wendung zum Führerstaat, Ideologische Komponenten in der politischen Philosophie Carl Schmitts*, Cologne 1958.

43. In my judgement the best examination is to be found in Hasso Hofmann, *Legitimität und Legalität, Der Weg der politischen Philosophie Carl Schmitts* (1964), 2nd edn Berlin 1992 (with a very valuable 'foreword' in which the author discusses the Schmitt literature).

44. See the two articles first quoted in note 10 and the author's essay: 'Legitimität' und 'Legalität' als Kategorien der staatlichen Existenz, in K. Held and J. Hennigfeld (eds), *Kategorien der Existenz, Festschrift für W. Janke*, Würzburg 1994, p. 415 *passim*.

45. Helmut Quaritsch (ed.), *Complexio Oppositorum, Über Carl Schmitt*, Berlin 1986, Preface 5.

46. Two books should be mentioned: *Heinrich Meier, Carl Schmitt, Leo Strauss und 'Der Begriff des Politischen', Zu einem Dialog unter Abwesenden*, Stuttgart 1988; Heinrich Meier, *Die Lehre Carl Schmitts, Vier Kapitel zur Unterscheidung Politischer Theologie und Politischer Philosophie*, Stuttgart 1994.

47. Miss Kennedy's original article: 'Carl Schmitt und die "Frankfurter Schule", Deutsche Liberalismuskritik im 20. Jahrhundert', *Geschichte und Gesellschaft* 12 (1986), p. 320 *passim*; the three critical articles: A. Söllner, 'Jenseits von Carl Schmitt, Wissenschaftsgeschichtliche Richtigstellungen zur politischen Theorie im Umkreis der "Frankfurter Schule"', *Geschichte und Gesellschaft* 12 (1986), p. 502 *passim*; M. Jay, '*Les extremes ne se touchent pas*, Eine Erwiderung auf E. Kennedy', *Geschichte und Gesellschaft* 13 (1987), p. 542 *passim*, UK Preuß, 'Carl Schmitt und die Frankfurter Schule, Deutsche Liberalismuskritik im 20. Jahrhundert, Anmerkungen zu einem Aufsatz von Ellen Kennedy', in *Geschichte und Gesellschaft* 13 (1987), p. 400 *passim*; Miss Kennedy's rejoinder: 'Carl Schmitt and the Francfort School, A Rejoinder', in *Telos, A Quarterly of Critical Thought*, 73 (1987). See also: P. Haungs, 'Diesseits oder jenseits von Carl Schmitt? Zu einer Kontroverse um die 'Frankfurter Schule und Jürgen Habermas', in H. Meier *et al.* (eds), *Politik – Philosophie – Praxis, Festschrift für W. Hennis*, Stuttgart 1988, p. 526 *passim*; H. Becker, *Die Parlamentarismuskritik bei Carl Schmitt und Jürgen Habermas*, Berlin 1994; and the author's essay: 'Carl Schmitt unter einer amerikanischen Perspektive', *Göttingische Gelehrte Anzeigen* 246 (1994), p. 145 *passim*. The whole controversy is highly indicative for the style of German political discourse: it is not a discourse at all!

48. Jürgen Habermas, 'Sovereignty and the *Führerdemokratie*', *The Times*

Literary Supplement, 29 September 1986, p. 1054; in German: 'Der Schrecken der Autonomie, Carl Schmitt auf Englisch', in Jürgen Habermas, *Eine Art Schadensabwicklung, Kleine Politische Schriften* VI, Frankfurt a. Main 1987, p. 102.

49. See my article: 'Zwei Begriffe des Politischen?, Jürgen Habermas und die störrische Faktizität des Politischen', in *Politisches Denken*, Jahrbuch 1994, Stuttgart 1995, p. 175 *passim*.

50. Melvyn A. Hille (ed.), *Hannah Arendt: The Recovery of the Public World*, New York 1979, p. 328 *passim*.

51. Jürgen Habermas, 'Nachholende Revolution und linker Diskursbedarf, Was heißt Sozialismus heute?', in Jürgen Habermas, *Die nachholende Revolution, Kleine Politische Schriften* VII, Frankfurt a. Main 1990, p. 188.

52. See the author's article: 'Hannah Arendt bei den Linken', in *Neue Politische Literatur*, 1993, p. 361 *passim*.

53. My article: 'Deutschland – aber wo liegt es?', in *liberal, Vierteljahreshefte für Politik und Kultur* 35 (1993), p. 8 *passim*.

54. A selection: Dieter Henrich, *Eine Republik Deutschland, Reflexionen auf dem Weg aus der deutschen Teilung*, Frankfurt a. Main 1990; Rüdiger Bubner, *Zwischenrufe, Aus den bewegten Jahren*, Frankfurt a. Main 1993; P. Braitling and W. Reese-Schäfer (eds), *Universalismus, Nationalismus und die neue Einheit der Deutschen, Philosophen und die Politik*, Frankfurt a. Main 1991.

55. Ralf Dahrendorf, 'Angst vor der Nation', in *liberal, Vierteljahreshefte für Politik und Kultur* 32 (1990), 85 *passim*.

HORST ALBERT GLASER

From the Tabula Rasa to the Rediscovery of the Nation. Tendencies in Post-War German Literature

I shall begin with a longish quotation, about which I shall make some comments:

The train in which we are sitting displaces the air as it did a year ago. The flak wagon is even streamlined, but in reality its sides are dented, its front squashed in. The faces on the station platforms make you want to pull the blinds down as quickly as possible. Fortunately most of them have no idea what sort of train this is. [. . .] Most of the information we get is already out of date; we have missed the connection; we are later every minute, and even if we arrive in Görlitz on time this evening, that is only a façade. We fall further and further behind, and we won't catch up, however much we turn one administrative district after another into an operational area and have the Home Guard build defences for us to fall back on. Our strides are too short; we can't catch up. Like a fire-brigade called too late we rush here and we rush there to the source of the flames, confer with the local bankers, incite them against each other; but in reality we cannot help. And then on to the next fire, and we order the district commanders and the bosses to appear, and someone is moved round, and a few changes are made, perhaps, at the top, and on we go again, always further, always faster. The refrigeration truck has broken down, and so has the news wagon; all we have got is a knapsack transmitter. In the command relay office people are getting on each other's nerves. Bully is winded, Bonnie has lost her bone, the Colonel is working in an oxygen mask and Mimmie's apron has been torn to shreds in the slipstream; the Wambke girl has typed out the notes for a speech on a train-timetable; the Reichs-railway director has no idea where we are. And what is this endless tunnel and those green lamps they're waving at

59

us? How many engines have we actually got up front? One would have been enough, that's for certain. And the tunnel has strange acoustics: someone's playing the *Deutschlandlied* on a Wurlitzer organ – at least it sounds like that [. . .][1]

The apocalyptic situation enshrines the last days of the Third Reich. The Russian armies are on the border, bombing missions are being flown against the towns, and the once so perfectly organized dictatorship is slowly falling apart. *Führers Hauptquartier* (Hitler's central command), as it was known, has been put on board a train that commences to rush hither and thither across the territory of the Reich, attempting to hold a crumbling bulwark here, to save the situation there. We are in this train, for the author of the passage belongs to the staff of the *Führers Hauptquartier*. The text *Im Sonderzug des Führers* ('In the *Führer's* Special Train'), from which I have been quoting, was typed by Felix Hartlaub in this very train. It was Hartlaub's job as a writer, along with others, to keep what was known as the Headquarters War Diary. In this Diary every phase and every movement of the Second World War was noted down as it came in from dispatches from the front and from the minutes of decisions made in Central Command. But Hartlaub, who had a Ph.D. in history as well as being a writer, kept a private diary alongside the official War Diary, and this private diary tells the story of the war, not in its strategic perspective but as a daily reality: the reality of a *Führer's* Headquarters that thought itself to be conducting a war which it no longer in any way controlled. The web of illusions fostered by those in charge – and it was an elevated world of madness that they inhabited, thinking all the time that the reins were still in their hands – this is something that Hartlaub not only sees through: he describes it with profound and subtle irony. If his diary had been found on him, he would have been shot outright for 'demoralization of the troops'. The diary ends where the quotation ends: we do not know whether its author continued writing, or even what happened in the tunnel. In the last days of the defence of Berlin, Hartlaub was sent down to the infantry; he was not heard of again. Almost certainly, somewhere under the ruins of that bombed and shot-up city, he has found an unknown grave.

If one reads the passage 'In the *Führer's* Special Train' as an allegory, the fall of the Third Reich appears in the guise of a gigantic railway accident. Everyone is in this train and no one knows where it is going – least of all those who think they have decided on the route.

In the train people hold meetings, debate, drink, make love and celebrate, while out there the world breaks into small pieces. Finally the train races across a viaduct or into a tunnel, everyone in it loses their sense of direction and we see nothing more. The image of the train crash is symptomatic of political catastrophe, for the railway system presupposes intact infrastructures and precise organization. It is, indeed, a quint-essence of the social mechanism itself, in which all things run according to a pre-ordained plan. If the plan breaks down – because wars do not run as they are supposed to – the machine of state crashes, its train is derailed.

It is no surprise, therefore, that the image of the railway accident is used by other authors too, to depict the catastrophe of 1945. It was particularly close to people in those last days of the war, when a chaotic transmigration began. Before the advancing Russian soldiers, not only the inhabitants of the German Eastern Territories fled, seeking out the centre of the *Reich*; they were joined by a stream of retreating troops, deserters and the remnants of dissolved and dissolving armies. When they were not on foot, they hung on to overfilled trains – so long as the rails were still intact and the engines had coal. But the engines often broke down too, or were hit by bombs; so trains had to be changed. But the new trains were generally going somewhere else, somewhere unplanned, because the old tracks had been destroyed. Out of this final chaos the image of a railway disaster grew with inevitable logic.

In his short prose text *Leviathan*, Arno Schmidt describes a sequence of days in February 1945: certainly a piece of literary fiction, but not far removed from the report of the war-diarist Hartlaub. A train makes its way through unknown country; attacking aircraft frequently force it to stop. In it sit refugees, deserters, children with bazookas in their hands: a miserable collection of humanity crushed by the machinery of war:

6.18
It's all over.
We rolled on, only a few hundred metres and we were on the viaduct. It drummed and echoed. Good that we could only go so slowly. High up over the river. Then suddenly the wagon was flung forward. Stood still again. The front bulkhead burst open. Everything happened so fast. We scurried out as carefully as we could. The arch of the bridge in front of us was missing; the engine dangled crookedly over the abyss (and behind us the sleeper-hook[2] had ripped up the track!!). Fire broke out of its exploded

boiler, and straight away the shells started singing in the air around us
(nice target, eh?!). They felt their way out (shouting against the howling
darkness) back along the body of the naked giant – there were no
railings. (Someone might have fallen, for there was a sudden scream like
a thunderbolt descending.) There! A jagged fire-storm stood roaring at
the other end. We (Anne and I) crept numbly (with racing hearts) into
the wagon. Iron demons wailed and shrilled around us, above us, below
us. The blows still crashed down in quick succession behind us, and once
everything shook as if a mountain were collapsing (and the water gurgled
and frothed). [. . .] Eight short paces behind the hook a muddy pool of fog
silently yawned. I picked up two ballast stones from the track and threw
one of them over the edge: there was not even a plop, nothing stirred,
sightlessness. With a fist of stone I flung the other: dumbly moaning it
fell away to the far bank. Listen. Nothing. I nodded stupidly, mysteriously.
Good, good. I turned back; I climbed into the wreck of the wagon, I said
to Anne: 'It's been hit behind as well. We are alone, in the middle of the
river, high above it.'[3]

One sees how closely Schmidt's apocalypse of the Third Reich
resembles Hartlaub's. Where the *'Führer's* special train' vanishes
from sight into a tunnel from which it never emerges, Schmidt's
refugee train hangs precariously on a viaduct that has been blown up
both in front of it and behind. The railway disaster is where the train
of history terminates, although the Third Reich wanted to take it to
a quite different destination – that of world power.

The catastrophe of 1945 was a terminus in many senses for the
young writers whose work began shortly before or after that date.
The year 1945 meant not only the end of a state and a social order,
but also the end of a literature that, in whichever way, was rooted in
the old order. In this respect the end was widely felt to harbour the
possibility of a new beginning. After the end of the old world and its
writing, a new world and new writing was called for: a situation that
soon took on its own name – *tabula rasa*, or *Kahlschlag* (clean sweep).
That too is the inner meaning of *Der Ruf* (the call), which became the
title of a periodical founded by a group of young men who had begun
to write as prisoners-of-war in England and America. They wanted to
gather a new generation of German writers from the homeward-
drifting stragglers; and they wanted, too, to call up out of the ashes a
new and better state founded on a new order. *Der Ruf* had a political
as well as a literary programme. It was to promote a new literature
of accuracy and truth, and at the same time to establish the political
premisses on which this could be built. Alfred Andersch and Hans
Werner Richter, the two editors of the magazine, saw Germany's

political future in a socialist order: they meant by this not a Stalinist dictatorship, nor Marxist dogmatism, but a freedom-loving socialism, not further to be defined. Andersch and Richter, however, could not proclaim their political ideals for very long in the pages of their magazine. The American forces of occupation, who had granted *Der Ruf* its licence, threatened to withdraw this licence if the liberal socialists continued to edit it. The publisher changed the editors, but this brought no better luck, and a few years later the magazine folded.

More forcibly than in the leading articles of *Der Ruf*, whose aim was more political than literary, the *Kahlschlag* or *tabula rasa* thesis apropos the new writing was maintained by the poet Wolfgang Weyrauch. Because the new literature has no literary history behind it, it can take on, freed from the ballast of history, the real things and objects which it faces. That means – once more – the quest for a new realism, a new form of objectivity or *Sachlichkeit*, unencumbered by memories of the old *Neue Sachlichkeit* of the 1920s. In the Afterword to the anthology *Tausend Gramm* (A Thousand Grams) we read:

> The men of the *Kahlschlag* [...] are writing the primer of the new German prose. They lay themselves open to the scorn of the snobs and the suspicion of both nihilists and optimists: oh, these people write like this because they cannot do any better. But the men of the 'clean sweep' know – or at least they sense – that the only method and the only intention that can regenerate our country's prose is that of the pioneer. The method of stocktaking. The intention of truth. Both at the cost of poeticism. Literature begins where existence begins. When the wind is blowing through the house, you have to ask why it is doing so. Beauty is a fine thing. But beauty without truth is bad. Truth without beauty is better. It paves the way for legitimate beauty. [...] The writers of the *Kahlschlag* [...] fix reality. Because they do so in the name of truth, they do not take photographs. They make X-rays. Their precision is surgical. Their reporting is antiseptic.[4]

One might think that in a land as destroyed as Germany was in the mid-1940s there would not be much left to X-ray. Reality had been so heavily X-rayed by bombs that only ruins were left. But in the midst of this destruction we see an author who looks round and lists what is left to him from the treasure-house of German culture. They are sad relics, but he can count on them. If he has ten or twelve things now, those things can multiply, and with the talents of a Robinson Crusoe he might build a new world out of them once more.

Weyrauch quotes a poem whose speaker is assuring himself, item after item, of what remains of his worldly goods, as if this could be the foundation for a new, secure existence. It is the famous poem *Inventur* (Inventory) by Günter Eich, which I shall quote first in the original and then in the translation by Michael Hamburger:

> Dies ist meine Mütze,
> dies ist mein Mantel,
> hier mein Rasierzeug
> im Beutel aus Leinen.
>
> Konservenbüchse:
> mein Teller, mein Becher,
> ich hab in das Weißblech
> den Namen geritzt.
>
> Geritzt hier mit diesem
> kostbaren Nagel,
> den vor begehrlichen
> Augen ich berge.
>
> Im Brotbeutel sind
> ein Paar wollene Socken
> und einiges, was ich
> niemand verrate,
>
> so dient er als Kissen
> nachts meinem Kopf.
> Die Pappe liegt hier
> zwischen mir und der Erde.
>
> Die Bleistiftmine
> lieb ich am meisten:
> tags schreibt sie mir Verse,
> die nachts ich erdacht.
>
> Dies ist mein Notizbuch,
> dies meine Zeltbahn,
> dies ist mein Handtuch,
> dies ist mein Zwirn.

Michael Hamburger's translation reads:

This is my cap,
this is my greatcoat,
and here's my shaving kit
in its linen bag.

A can of meat:
my plate, my mug,
into its tin
I've scratched my name.

Scratched it with this
invaluable nail
which I keep hidden
from covetous eyes.

My bread bag holds
two woollen socks
and a couple of things
I show to no one,

like that it serves me
as a pillow at night.
Between me and the earth
I lay this cardboard.

This pencil lead
is what I love best:
by day it writes verses
I thought up in the night.

This is my notebook
and this is my groundsheet,
this is my towel,
this is my thread.

One could use a concept from the music-history of the 1980s and
call this poetry of extreme reduction 'minimal literature'. Frugality
of speech characterized not only the poetry of the immediate post-
war period; it also characterized its prose, if we look at the work of

many young writers like Arno Schmidt, whose earliest work, *Leviathan*, I mentioned earlier. Wolfgang Borchert's is another name one cannot pass over: that great hope of post-war German literature who died in 1947 at the age of 26. Where Eich looks at things, Borchert looks at people, at mankind. Indeed he tries to look further still: tries to discern whether somewhere above man or somewhere behind there may be a figure lurking whom we could call God. His gaze travels despondently round, for – to paraphrase Brecht – no God is in sight. And this Godless space transforms into a meaningless vacuum occupied by indifferent bodies, more like corpses than people. A waiting-room, where four such figures wait for a train, presents a ghost-picture of a state after death:

> They hung on the chairs. They hung across the tables. Suspended there by a frightful tiredness. In the face of this tiredness there was no sleep. It was tiredness with the world, and it expected nothing. At the most a train. And in a waiting-room. And there they hung, suspended over chairs and across tables. They hung in their clothes and in their skin, as if they were tired of them, the clothes. And the skin. They were ghosts and they had dressed up in this costume-skin, and for a time they were playing man. They hung on their skeletons like scarecrows on their poles. Suspended by life to the mockery of their own brains and to the torment of their hearts. And every wind played to them. Played with them. They hung in a sort of life, suspended there by a God with no face.[5]

From here to Beckett's *Endgame* is not a big step. In hindsight it is astonishing that this 'prose of misery' could be called new realism. After all, for Beckett's terminal condition the 1960s invented the concept of 'absurd' prose. But when the conditions described are themselves absurd, their description might count as realistic.

It was Gustav René Hocke who in the pages of *Der Ruf* advocated this sort of minimal writing as the 'prose of reduced circumstances'. New prose writing should describe in all its bareness 'what one finds at the edge of the ruins and the tracks'.[6] One should see things as they are and speak of them 'with courage'. 'In the ruins you will discover the first new laws of present-day sociological and psychological reality, above all the unambiguity and the simplicity of suffering'.[7] The 'inflated, artistic [or also artificial] prose' of past epochs must end its calligraphic exercises, its devotion to fine writing, and turn its attention to 'things'. Only in this way can real language flow again out of the 'baffling artefacts of nothingness': language that utters 'reality, bright, clear [and] sharp'. In short, the 'new realism' in writing must dispense with classical 'beauty'. For in that dimension all one sees is the care with which words are chosen to form 'well-rounded periods' with their 'euphonious' rhythms. 'But what is actually being said? You understand: said!'. For Hocke, probably nothing. This 'language of the educated seminary' no longer speaks to us, and we shall have no more truck with it. In place of 'calligraphy' we need perception of reality, or, to put it the other way round: 'In the face of suffering, beauty adjusts her proportions.'[8] When fine writing falsifies 'suffering', then beauty in all her finery must be assaulted.

That was Gottfried Benn's view too – one of the pre-war generation of writers whom Hocke had dismissed as 'calligraphers'. Sitting in the ruins of Berlin after the catastrophe, Benn caricatured the place where he worked and wrote, calling it a 'Beauty Salon', a place where one went to have one's warts and spots removed. The comparison of the writer's study to a cosmetic institute was particularly appropriate in his case, for both before the war and after it Benn earned his living as a specialist for skin and venereal diseases. If he had had to live on his income as a writer he would have starved as a very young man. He later calculated that he had earned scarcely more than two marks eighty a month from his pen. He had had no inclination after the war to reopen his medical practice, and none to write 'beautiful poems'. In the *Berlin Novelle* of 1947 that he entitled *Der Ptolomäer* (Ptolemaic Man), the great 'cosmic destroyer' of German literature imagines himself installing a machine-gun in his 'beauty salon', in order to shoot down all those who come to him in search of health and beauty:

An evil winter is ending, one with continual relapses and continual new peaks, which regularly brought with them what they called a brightening up (evidently a very special moment on the scale of cheerfulness and brightness); a truly malign winter in the face of which every sacrifice of rudimentary furniture-scraps, children's cradles and flotsam from the ruins was made in vain; a winter that for four months drew blood at minus 20. Wolves on the Oder, eagles in the Müggelbergen [near Berlin]. A winter of occupation! The magistrature dug in behind the occupying forces, these behind the elements, these it seems behind the highlands of Tibet, these behind some Dalai Lama or other and so on – and in consequence everything broke down. The shops went to sleep, money vanished, taxes were left unpaid, life ground to a halt. My own business, beauty salon (varicose veins included) had long since ceased to function. The surgery was unheated for weeks. To risk putting an arm out of its fur-coat or a foot out of its rags would have brought the customer into new realms of pathology. I was glad. No more frozen pedals [i.e. feet], no more swollen fingers, itching bellies, varicose lumps front and back! Alone at last! In the end even the ringing and knocking on the door was too much. All probing questions notwithstanding, I had salvaged a machine-gun from the great struggle of the nations, and I secretly set this up to cover the street approach and shot down any suspicious figure. The bodies didn't look much different from those of the casually frozen or those who had finished off their own lives; they lay on the pavements, and passers-by thought that quite natural. Toothache or an inflamed pulp might have got them moving, but humps in the snow – that might be rats or old bed-cushions.[9]

If 'Ptolemaic Man' wanted to shoot down all those who at that inappropriate moment sought beauty, whether of the body or of literature, René Hocke was more modest, contending simply that the age of the *Calligrafisti* was past and that of the *Contenutisti* [viz those possessing content] was at hand. For Hocke, the *Calligrafisti* were in particular the authors of the so-called *Innere Emigration*: authors who had not left Germany under the 'Third Reich' and gone into 'outer' emigration, but had stayed and chosen the 'inner' variety. If they wanted to continue to publish under the pressure of censorship, but not to conform to the ruling ideology, then – as Hocke conceded quite fairly – they *could* only write esoterically. 'In many cases this strange esoteric style was by no means freely chosen. It arose out of an extreme caution and out of the desire to write without compromising oneself politically or falling foul of the wolfish censors.'[10] Naturally the vagueness and the cultivated esotericism of this language was not without effect on its content. For 'slowly but increasingly [...] the content of the utterance evaporated, leaving only the form, until in the end what remained was a masterly way with words without any real content at all'.[11] Who these *Calligrafisti* were supposed to be was never said. Hocke names no names. He might have meant Hausmann or Wiechert, perhaps.

It is tempting to extend the accusation of *calligraphism* to certain writers of the 'outer' emigration too. Hermann Broch and Thomas Mann tried – as also did Alfred Döblin – to present the German catastrophe as a tragedy of historical and philosophical proportions. In consciously epochal novels they reached far back into the past, in order to show the inevitability of the historical process; in doing so they made copious use of the stylistic device of allegory. In *Doktor Faustus* Thomas Mann brought up to date the late medieval saga, inventing the composer Adrian Leverkühn, who was supposed not only to have originated Schönberg's twelve-tone scale and to have relived the biography of Nietzsche in his madness, but over and above all this to have entered into a pact with Satan. Leverkühn is in truth an overdeveloped allegorical figure who stands for so much that it is at times unclear where he stands himself. Broch's *Tod des Vergil* ('The Death of Virgil') stretches still further back into the past, seeing in the fall of the Roman Republic a mirror of the fall of German culture.

However gripping they may be in their individual scenes or figures, these historico-philosophical novels must in the end be judged failures. Not that they are any more so than is Brecht's farce about the 'Rise and Rise of Arturo Ui', as the *Aufhaltsame Aufstieg des Arturo Ui* is known – wittily but perhaps inaccurately translated – in English. Brecht had attempted to dress up Hitler's career in a parable of mafia-crime and cauliflowers. One can only agree with Adorno's resigned comment that the incommensurability of German fascism can be expressed neither in the mode of crime fiction nor in that of allegorical myth.

I have mentioned some authors of both the 'inner' and the 'outer' forms of emigration in order to make clear that the young writers of the new 'realism' did not have the literary scene to themselves when they began to publish after 1945. If an account sheet were to be drawn up, the productivity of the older generation would indeed be seen to exceed that of the younger. But this was no fruitful contest or joint venture between two different ways of 'coming to terms with the past'; it was more a grudging or at most indifferent coexistence in space and time. The two parties had nothing to say to each other.

The situation was unchanged until the end of the 1950s, when another young generation began to write: a generation who had lived through the catastrophe of 1945 as children or adolescents, and could not, therefore, as Borchert or Schmidt had done, make their debut in *Trümmerprosa* – the 'prose of the ruins', as it was called. They wrote large, wide-ranging novels again, not however this time historical or philosophical or indeed allegorical constructs, but eloquent and imaginative depictions of a lost childhood. I refer to the Danzig novels of Günter Grass, Siegfried Lenz's stories of West Prussia and Horst Bienek's Gleiwitz tetralogy. What characterizes all these novels of memory is – despite their differences – the concern to reconstruct that lost childhood. They are, if one might use the phrase, a *Recherche du temps perdu* in German, and in clear deference to the *petit bourgeois* circumstances of their background. When authors set about remembering times past, the time of childhood is always gone; but when the childhood in question also belonged to a sunken culture – namely to that of the German eastern territories – then one can read Grass's *Blechtrommel* ('The Tin Drum'), Lenz's *Deutschstunde* ('German Lesson') or Bienek's *Erste Polka* ('First Polka') as *Heimat*-novels of a special kind.[12] Not for them the childhood paradise bathed in transfiguring light: they show quite clearly how home and childhood had been gambled away by their parents' generation. The Danzig of the common man, portrayed in the 'Tin Drum' in all its fantastic pandemonium: that town no longer exists, any more than does Bienek's Gleiwitz in Upper Silesia or the villages of the Masurian plain. These territories and their towns belong now to Poland: they are Polish, and nothing is left to recall the life of Germans there 50 or 60 years ago. The modern visitor to Pomerania or Silesia realizes not without shock what that 'vanitas' means, about which the authors of the Silesian Baroque so often wrote.

Reconstructions of a past life were also written by authors who left the German Democratic Republic in the 1960s and 1970s and settled in the Federal Republic. Many of them were forbidden to return, so that, like Uwe Johnson, they could go to New York but no longer to Leipzig. His reconstruction of the GDR is, however, not a memory of childhood but the attempt to write an anatomy of dictatorship – or of one particular dictatorship. Johnson's *Mutmaßungen über Jacob* ('Conjectures about Jacob'), or his *Dritte Buch über Achim* ('Third Book about Achim'), were long considered merely to be studies in the montage style of a 1920s novel. Today, after the collapse of the GDR, they read differently. Ever since we have learnt that the state security service of the GDR, the 'Stasi', had 10 per cent of the population under surveillance or spied on by other people, and that the case files they built up, stacked upright next to each other, fill a space 128 kilometres long – ever since this fact became known, Johnson's novels, with their disparate narrative levels, narrative perspectives and narrative discourses, seem to stem from nothing more stylistic than hundreds of spy-reports stuck haphazardly into files by an indifferent Stasi officer. Just as the Ministry for State Security never really knew what was going on in the population they so keenly observed, so the reader of 'Conjectures about Jacob' only gets a fragmentary picture of its protagonist, from which he or she cannot tell why the hero is actually run over by the train and what this might conceivably have meant for others.

Günter Grass and Siegfried Lenz would probably protest at my counting their early novels as *Heimat*-literature. The connection to those societies and groups of Germans expelled from their homes and from their native countries in the East would be too close: those Silesians, Pomeranians and West Prussians who still today insist on their right to return to what used to be German territory. It is not in any way my intention, of course, to associate these authors with the political ideology of the *Heimatvertriebenen*, the expellees, especially as both writers were and still are committed supporters of the treaties with the eastern European countries, in which very early on – as early as the 1970s – the post-war frontiers of Germany were accepted.

German literature of the last 30 years bears the stamp of many different authors and stylistic modes. Rather, however, than attempt a summary overview, I will retreat behind the thesis of Hanns-Josef Ortheil, who considers it a hopeless endeavour to collate such manifold phenomena under two or three headings:

> It would not be at all difficult to name at this juncture forty or fifty authors who have published more than one noteworthy, and in some cases far too little known work. But it would be impossible to group them successfully into a single 'trend' or stylistic movement. Most have long since developed their own poetics, and most of these poetics have little in common. We are in a situation of diversity, a full palette of different approaches that cannot be reduced to quickly assembled headlines.[13]

Literary affairs in Germany could have continued along their tranquil path, each writer pursuing his or her own poetics – Peter Handke a new migrant novel, Botho Strauß a new conversation-piece – if the peaceful, or perhaps indifferent, coexistence of the various modes had not been suddenly interrupted in 1989. The collapse of the GDR and its union with the Federal Republic sent an alarm through many a writer's study, startled many an armchair-dweller out of complacency. The politics that had, at the end of the 1980s, largely disappeared from the horizon of contemporary writers, returned to them – the older ones at least – in memories of their own beginnings in the 1960s, and they began once more to enter the political fray with articles and on discussion panels. These articles and interviews are all we have for the moment from the authors who espoused the cause of German unification: the novels and the plays will have to wait for a few years yet.

Whether or not the Germans should be one nation again – this question dominated the agenda, when in 1990 political developments concentrated on the accession of the GDR to the

Federal Republic. All sorts of warning voices rose – voices which wanted not the old GDR but socialism in the shape of a new GDR. In particular Günter Grass and Heiner Müller pursued the mirage of a 'third way' between the bankers' dictatorship of the Federal Republic and the one-party dictatorship of the Democratic Republic. That all of a sudden there should once more be a German national state – this had to be a shock to authors who had come to terms with partition and, for all their criticism, had settled comfortably into the federal way of life. In a sort of psychic automatism Grass associated the word 'nation' with the word 'nationalism', and the word 'nationalism' with 'National Socialism'. Or, in other words, whoever aspires to a single German state has forgotten the concentration camps of Auschwitz and will be guilty if anything like that should ever arise again. The bizarre thesis that Germans should be precluded from a unified state because they allowed the extermination camps of Auschwitz has been heavily criticized by other writers, in particular by Günter de Bruyn and Martin Walser. But Grass was unimpressed by the reproofs of his colleagues, and in 1992, in his *Rede vom Verlust* ('Speaking of Loss'), he again conjured up the spectre of a single fascist German state, drawing a direct line from Auschwitz to the pogroms of Rostock and Mölln. The tenor of the speech was simple: 'You've got the proof!'[14]

Whether the at times murderous violence against Turks, asylum-seekers and disabled people is explicable in terms of the accession of the GDR to the Federal Republic in 1990 is more than questionable. Martin Walser listened more attentively than Grass had done to the cries of the demonstrators, and realized that the *Deutschland*-shouts of the skinheads revealed a shortcoming: that of suppressed national sentiment. The idea of the nation had, precisely because of this suppression, been overcharged to mythical proportions – as if to shout *Heil* [which means 'healing' as well as 'hailing': trans.] would put an end to individual ills. I quote from an essay of Martin Walser's:

> When they pin the sentence 'I am proud to be a German' on their sleeve, those who feel sick at the sight should first ask themselves how that sentence came about. These things are not passed down. [. . .] If a person has nothing else to be proud of than his nationality, he is a poor fish of a German indeed. [. . .] I do not believe him. The nation is never the main point for anybody – has not been for a long time. [. . .] The sentence is a demonstration in itself, an imposing gesture. The people who hoist the flag in this way know that they hit and hurt us, and that, more than

anything else, is what they want. [. . .] These are the sentences and the actions of children who have grown up in a society that bracketed out all that was national or met it with unrestrained criticism. [. . .] The word 'nation' itself was only possible in the most reprobate of combinations: National-Socialism.[15]

Of course it is not the search for nationality that makes skinheads chase Turks. A number of ingredients combine to produce that witches' cauldron of violence. The taboo of national entity is invoked, Walser suggested, because of the total bankruptcy of state-based socialism. This has led to a crisis 'which hits the 15- to 25-year-olds harder than the rest'.[16] It is total bankruptcy that has produced the crisis, 'not German unification'.

So far I have said nothing of Hans Magnus Enzensberger, the tightrope-walker among German writers. He has, so far as I know, only spoken once in the debate on the national question. While Grass, Heiner Müller, Walser and de Bruyn disputed whether or not a German national state was desirable, Enzensberger pointed out that the citizens of that future entity already practised it – and did so without paying much heed to the concept of 'nation'. For what else did the 'masses' do, when they 'in their imperturbable scepticism simply ignored the slogans of the mighty and of their leader-writers'? They got promptly on with the work of 'clearing up', tackling with their own hands what was necessary, without waiting for the 'helpless apparatus of state [whether] on this side [of the old border] or that':

> The village mayor, who on his own initiative had the deserted road and the broken bridge repaired; the carpenter who got the circular saw going again across the border [. . .] And so far as standing upright is concerned, those who practised it most clearly were those who, ignoring the state and its powers, made their way over the border, groaning under the weight of their plastic bags, before 9 November 1989 and caused the German situation to break into a dance. Those border-crossers with the upright gait brought not the millennium but a simple everyday that needs no prophets.[17]

The process that Enzensberger describes may console the prophets of nationhood or of the socialist *internationale*, or it may not. At the end of the twentieth century the concept of nation has, for Germans, no further role to play. What matters is work, housing, pensions – not a great deal more, and not much less either. For the rest, Germans are waiting for Europe – but nobody knows yet what sort of song that will be or what writing it will bring. To some it is already a foretaste of utopia, to others a tragic farce. Perhaps those will be right who expect no song at all, but the mumbo-jumbo of bureaucrats talking over each others' heads. Botho Strauß would be the author for that sort of comedy of functionaries, where guests stand and talk at interminable parties till they drop with tiredness, while things outside go on on their uninterpretable course.

Notes

1. Felix Hartlaub, 'Tagebuch aus dem Kriege', in *Das Gesamtwerk. Dichtungen – Tagebücher*, Frankfurt am Main, 1955, pp. 195–6.
2. A huge steel hook, called *Schwellenreißer* ('sleeper-ripper'), attached to the last truck on the train. It destroyed the track by ripping up the sleepers behind it as the train went along.
3. Arno Schmidt, *Leviathan*, Zurich 1985, pp. 26–7.
4. Wolfgang Weyrauch, 'Kahlschlag', *Mit dem Kopf durch die Wand. Geschichten, Gedichte, Essays und ein Hörspiel 1929–1977*, Darmstadt and Neuwied, 1977, p. 51.
5. Wolfgang Borchert, 'Der Kaffee ist undefinierbar' ['The Coffee is Indefinable'], *Das Gesamtwerk*, Hamburg, 1986, 195.
6. Gustav René Hocke, 'Deutsche Kalligraphie oder Glanz und Elend der modernen Literatur' ['German Calligraphy, or the Splendour and Misery of Modern Literature'], *Der Ruf*, Vol. I, No. 7, p. 10.
7. Ibid., p. 9.
8. Ibid., p. 10.
9. Gottfried Benn, 'Der Ptolomäer', *Gesammelte Werke in acht Bänden*, ed. Dieter Wellershoff, Vol. 5, Munich, 1975, pp. 1377–8.
10. Gustav René Hocke, *Deutsche Kalligraphie*, p. 9.
11. Ibid.
12. Heimatromane, like the *Heimat* – films popular in the 1950s and 1960s, were sentimental novels set in the various regions of Germany and playing on the sense of local roots.
13. Hanns-Josef Ortheil, *Schauprozesse. Beiträge zur Kultur der achtziger Jahre*, Munich, 1990, p. 179.
14. Günter Grass, *Rede vom Verlust. Über den Niedergang der politischen Kultur im geeinten Deutschland*, Göttingen, 1992.
15. Martin Walser, *Der Spiegel*, 26, 1993, p. 41.
16. Ibid., p. 45.
17. Hans Magnus Enzensberger, *Frankfurter Allgemeine Zeitung*, 19.5.1990, p. 2 of the Sunday Supplement.

KURT SONTHEIMER

Intellectuals in the Political Life of the Federal Republic of Germany

Whenever intellectuals talk about intellectuals, they are likely to be suspected of seeing the group to which they feel themselves to belong in a rather one-sided and flattering manner. This is particularly the case when dealing with the issue of the role of intellectuals in politics, because politics – the realm of power – is one of the most important aspects of intellectual discourse and criticism. The tendency is, however, mitigated by the fact that intellectuals are by no means homogeneous. There are left-wing intellectuals and right-wing intellectuals, who usually oppose each other, and between them is a vaguely defined group of so-called liberal intellectuals who claim to be free and independent in their judgement. They believe that they represent the freedom of the intellect and that they are only bound by the requirements of the intellect, which, in turn, has its own rules and standards.

If I were to position myself on the extremely wide scale of intellectual tendencies, I would probably be somewhere on the centre-left. This is not a particularly precise characterization, but it does allow one to evolve one's views in reaction to a changing intellectual and political environment. These comments may make it easier to make sense of the following analysis of the role of intellectuals in German politics – it is an analysis which I have attempted to make as objective as possible, but which necessarily relies to a certain extent on subjective interpretation.

When I speak of intellectuals, I do not mean the large numbers of people who belong to the academic and technical intelligentsia, and who are employed by purely functional economic and social organizations. Such people do not usually enjoy the freedom to articulate their opinions independently to the public.

Genuine intellectuals are only those who have no organizational commitments, who articulate their ideas on public issues and who assess critically issues of public concern and the actions or negligence of those in power. Their right to criticize is legitimized by their belief that intellectual freedom is for the good of humanity and by their subjective interpretation of the significance of the free intellect and of intellectual dialogue for positive societal development. They claim to belong to those who possess a special sensibility for the fundamental political and intellectual values of society. On the basis of this sensibility, and the responsibility that intellectuals bear for the good of society, they believe that it is legitimate to exercise criticism and to place the holders of power in the dock before their critical intellect. Because their criticisms are publicly aired, they are exercising the functions of public office, without having been elected or appointed by anybody. They allow themselves the freedom to challenge those in power with the intention of thus contributing to societal improvement. The powerful can listen to this criticism; they can possibly react to it, or they can simply ignore it. In contemporary democracy, this is usually dependent on the level of pressure which intellectuals are able – with the help of public opinion – to exert. The criticisms which are made by independent intellectuals are nearly always ineffective. In other words, the intellectuals are powerless when they face those who have power. They then like to complain about this impotence of intellect – but this isn't a scientific law or something which is necessarily inevitable. Again and again, we see situations in which intellectual criticism attains autonomous power. Intellectuals have an advantage over those they feel compelled to criticize – the intellectual is not required to act politically in the sense that he must make concrete decisions. The politician is always caught in a particular constellation of power which determines his actions. The intellectual, on the other hand, is an independent spirit who does not have to consider such constellations because he does not have to make decisions himself.

This argument – which was first propagated by Joseph Schumpeter – played a significant role in Germany in the 1970s amongst those who were critical of the left-wing intelligentsia. An example is the conservative sociologist Helmut Schelsky in his book

Die Arbeit tun die anderen. Klassenkampf und Priesterherrschaft der Intellektuellen ('Let the Others do the Work. Class Struggle and Theocracy of the Intellectuals').[1] In this book, he attacks the predominance of left-wing intellectuals on the German political scene during and after the student revolts. During the early years of the Federal Republic and during the era of Adenauer, it wasn't yet possible, however, to speak of such predominance.

The history of the role of intellectuals in the Federal Republic can be divided into four phases which run parallel to the political development of Germany's second republic:

1. the intellectuals in the wilderness (the Adenauer era);
2. the intellectuals in proximity to power (1968 and its consequences);
3. the process of intellectual and political change (from Schmidt to Kohl);
4. the muted intellectuals (the period of unification); and
5. unavailing self-contemplation (contemporary German intellectuals).

Such divisions are of course rather arbitrary, since intellectual developments are not primarily dependent on political conditions. They do, however, facilitate a clear structuring of the material and a historically-oriented appraisal of the key issues in the intellectual and political development of the Federal Republic.

I. The Intellectuals in the Wilderness – The Adenauer Era

To categorize German intellectuals as a group who share the same views and objectives is as difficult to do as it is in any other Western country. It was, however, always a characteristic of the Federal Republic that the label 'Intellectual' was only applied to those writers and publicists who either classified themselves or were perceived as left-wing. It is noteworthy that no group of right-wing intellectuals that could make a significant impact on public life ever appeared. Of course, there were and are a number of right-oriented professors, critics and publicists in the Federal Republic, but they were not the ones who were usually meant when people spoke of intellectuals.

The absence of a significant intellectual critical potential on the right wing is one of the most striking and historically significant differences between the intellectual–political situations under the Bonn and the Weimar Republics. In Weimar, the intelligentsia were either on the Left or on the Right but hardly in the Centre; in Bonn the intelligentsia are, indeed, somewhat to the Left, but the left-wing positions taken up until the end of the 1960s, and thus the beginning of the student revolts, were moderate and liberal compared to the stance of the left-wing intellectuals of Weimar. On the other hand, the nationalist, conservative-revolutionary tradition of the Weimar Republic did not – if we exclude a few peripheral phenomena – express itself under Bonn. Instead, there was an attempt to cultivate a relatively moderate liberal conservatism which emphasized the value of the political centre. Compared with the extreme polarization between communism and fascism and between rationalism and irrationality which were characteristic of the Weimar Republic, and which contributed to its enormous tension and disunity, the political and intellectual spectrum in the Federal Republic was initially strikingly narrow. It was defined by positions which would have been perceived as centrist in the Weimar period, but for which at that time, and to the detriment of that Republic, German intellectuals had little time. This is at least a partial explanation for the tragic failure of a republic whose intellectual élite, apart from a few exceptions such as Thomas Mann, were not prepared to play a constructive role in supporting the new democratic state.

The peculiarities of the intellectual evolution of the Federal Republic cannot be understood without analysing the state of consciousness present at the end of the war amongst those members of the intelligentsia who had not sympathized with National Socialism. It is true that the 'German catastrophe' did function as a trigger mechanism for contemplation and analysis as to how the German Reich could have ended as it did and, more importantly, how the National Socialist takeover could ever have happened in the first place. At the same time, however, this disaster was perceived by many post-war intellectuals as a chance to leave the terrible past behind them and to begin something new. For the young generation of intellectuals who were debating the intellectual and political future during the time of defeat and occupation, German history, which had come to a temporary end anyway in the total defeat of 1945, offered virtually no starting-points or lines of continuity. It was not considered useful to adopt either the ill-fated Weimar Republic or earlier periods of German history as models. Hence after defeat came the birth of the historically inappropriate concept of the *Stunde Null* or 'Zero Hour', in which there was a conscious attempt to turn away from the past, to lay new intellectual foundations and to begin a new form of political life based on legality and democratic freedom.

Unlike the younger left-wing intellectuals, those conservatively-oriented writers who were still popular after the war (Reinhold Schneider, Hans Zehrer, Ernst Jünger, Werner Bergengruen and others) looked for the causes of the German disaster rather more in the 'blackest depths of history', in the terrible alienation of the Germans from the values of humanist tradition, in the 'loss of the centre' (Sedlmayer) and in religion. Their objective was to set the image of the human being 'back up straight' after it had been so brutally destroyed and damaged by the National Socialists. Those young intellectuals who saw themselves as left-wing were less interested in the role of metaphysics and the renewal of religious ties. After the collapse, they envisaged a new form of social order which – without hesitation – they called socialism, and which for them involved a symbiosis of social justice, solidarity and the concept of freedom. As a consequence of their experience of the Weimar Republic, they believed that democracy, justice and solidarity could not prosper on the foundations of a capitalist economic order. For left-wing intellectuals of the early period, *Demokratischer Sozialismus* (democratic socialism) became the defining feature of the new order that was to emerge from the ruins of the Third Reich. This socialism was rather idealistic, and its theoretical characteristics were rather vague. The decisive factor in the thinking of left-wing intellectuals after the war was, however, the emphasis on the democratic and constitutional elements of socialism. This necessitated a decisive rejection of Soviet-style socialism, which was seen as a perversion of socialist values. German left-wing intellectuals called for a constructive partnership between planning and freedom. One of their spokesmen was Hans Werner Richter, who published the journal *Der Ruf*, a journal typical of this tendency in post-war thought, and who later became the mentor of the literary *Group 47*. He expressed the problem as follows:

> Yes to socialism and freedom! No to the subordination of one by the other! Subordination of freedom by socialist planning means renewed enslavement, it means military barracks, concentration camps, gallows

and war. Subordination of planning to liberal freedom on the other hand means the continuation of hunger and of the mass suffering and death which we are now experiencing. The young generation is socialist. What it is searching for is the fulfilment of human need within a stable socialist order.

Deep mistrust towards all ideologies and towards the old political slogans was a characteristic feature of the fundamental philosophy shared by young left-wing intellectuals in the emerging Federal Republic. The fact that political parties were forming again in the Western zones which, in their opinion, were building on the same ideological foundations as they had before the Third Reich, led them to the belief that the old system was re-establishing itself. They were of the opinion that the old party-political groups and their representatives were not in a position to lead the intellectual and political renewal of Germany. Instead, they believed that the young people who had experienced the war should take on this task. Only they could create a new Germany.

From the beginning of the 1950s the expression 'Restoration', which had been popularized by the left-wing Catholic publicist Walter Dirks, became the dominant critical buzz-word amongst left-wing intellectuals. Restoration signified the thoughtless re-imposition of the old order instead of a new beginning based on fresh intellectual foundations. It manifested itself in the predominance of politicians like Konrad Adenauer, Kurt Schumacher and Theodor Heuß, whose definitive experiences had been during the Weimar era and who had apparently not learnt much else new in the meantime. Restoration was, critically, also the re-establishment of the old social and economic order.

Under the spell of this restoration critique, the intellectuals soon began to agonize over the discrepancies between power and intellect as they had done during the Weimar period. This is because those in power were not doing and saying what the intellectuals expected from them. As the representatives of a progressive and democratic spirit, they felt as though they had been abandoned again by those in power. More and more, they had the impression that nobody listened to them, that their criticisms were not heeded and that their continuous interference in public affairs was regarded as disruptive. They experienced the Federal Republic as a state in which the free, independent intellect was little valued. They believed that the economy, the large societal interest groups and the established parties completely dominated the scene, and that these groups assigned the intellectuals nothing more than a subservient or secondary role.

This widespread emotional condition amongst German intellectuals made it difficult for them to identify with the Federal Republic more strongly. Their critique of the system was, however, quite moderate. There was no animosity, but instead a diffuse feeling of disquiet and a degree of resignation.

II. The Intellectuals in Proximity to Power (1968 and its Consequences)

During the course of the 1960s, this situation changed noticeably. The radicalization of a part of the German intellectual scene was, however, less an autonomous development than a reaction to the student protest movement, with which many intellectuals became involved. Thus a radical intellectual potential was able to develop within just a few years which was decisively to contribute to the uncertainty and the radicalization of political consciousness. The forms of action adopted by the students were unheard of in the Federal Republic – demonstrations, sit-ins, limited forms of illegality, the use of violence, etc. It was this force of student protest that drove many intellectuals to engage in a radical critique of the system.

It is difficult to say exactly what moved a section of the West German intelligentsia to start digging up the ambiguous teachings of Marx that had been ignored for so long and then to apply them – in both dogmatic and non-dogmatic fashions – to contemporary conditions. It seems that the growing disquiet with the immobility of German politics in the 1960s led to a felt need for a radical change in course, together with an equally radical methodology of analysis and interpretation. In general terms, a more pressing need developed for universal theories. In its many different forms, Marxism provided the best intellectual scaffolding for this need.

The extent to which the intellectual situation of the country in the 1970s had become a serious concern is demonstrated by a speech of the then Federal President Walter Scheel in 1977. On the occasion of the 500th anniversary of Tübingen university, Scheel condemned the contemporary left-wing intellectual critique of the Federal Republic with the following words:

Government, Parliament, trade unions, the courts, the bureaucracy, the economy and the universities themselves are ridiculed and placed under suspicion. Everything which they achieve is rejected. They are presented as enemies of the people who should be attacked. At the same time, the people making these accusations present themselves in radiant purity and as the very epitome of devoted engagement and high intellect. This is an amazingly simplistic view of the world, in which good and evil are clearly identified. It is quite untouched by any notion of serious criticism, the main task of which is to differentiate that which at first glance appears simple. But it is completely devoid of genuine critical faculty. It is exaggerated criticism, it is criticism without self-criticism by people who think that they have a monopoly on the truth. It is therefore also an undemocratic form of criticism.

I also took part in 1976 in the castigation of the intellectuals with my book: *Das Elend unserer Intellektuellen* ('The Pitiful State of our Intellectuals').[2] Its basic tenet: I am convinced that more than a few West German intellectuals have misunderstood or even betrayed their task and function in a democratic state. How else is it possible that they portray our political system as depraved and inhuman when in fact it will stand up well in comparison with other political systems in the world, not only in the fields of welfare and security, but also freedom and respect for human rights? How else is it possible that progressive intellectuals have turned the 'crisis of legitimacy' of our democracy into such a prevalent topic in social science seminars, despite the fact that a genuine, deep-rooted crisis of legitimacy is nowhere to be seen? How else is it possible that in certain left-wing intellectual circles the Federal Republic is characterized as a bourgeois state moving with unstoppable momentum towards fascism?[3] This is now history, but it has left its mark on the intellectual and political life of the Federal Republic.

The years preceding and after 1968 were, without doubt, the high point of intellectual influence on German politics. By the 1960s, leading writers were publicly calling on people to vote for the SPD with Willy Brandt at its head. For the 1969 election, which led to the transfer of power, Günter Grass founded a social democratic electoral society. Many leading intellectuals joined this and were successful in their promotion of the SPD. The transfer of power, which was deemed so vitally necessary by liberal and left-wing intellectuals, was completed and led, in turn, to a temporary reconciliation of intellect and power. Brandt was the first Federal Chancellor to recognize officially the Union of German Authors and to appeal to the intellectuals to participate actively in the reform of German democracy. The relationship between the government and the intellectuals had never been as harmonious as during the five years of Brandt's political office.

This honeymoon was, however, fragile and could not last. On the one hand, because the intellectuals were very far from being a homogeneous group. On the other hand, because the euphoria over the change of government rapidly disappeared and the replacement of Brandt by Schmidt meant that the intellectuals lost an important point of reference. A pragmatist, Helmut Schmidt was the embodiment of a quite different type of politician from the thoughtful, sensitive, visionary intellectual, Willy Brandt. Intellectuals are at the best of times very difficult to categorize as one group. In the 1960s they had – through their critique of the 'CDU state' – made quite a homogeneous impression. The years 1968 and 1969, however – the student revolts and the change of government, and the consequences of these events, led to a widespread dispersal of intellectual thought and to a new arrangement of the intellectual scene. There were the New Left intellectuals and their many followers who dominated the universities, and who, under the spell of critical theory and of the newly rediscovered Marxism, moved on from criticism to a fundamental questioning of capitalist society and Western democracy. There were the liberals who were in favour of reform, especially of the education system, but who now had to protect the principles of Western democracy which were so dear to them against left-wing revolutionaries and theoreticians. Then there were the conservatives who, until this time, had hardly made their presence felt as an intellectual force, but who now started to mobilize against the so-called cultural revolution which was taking place in Germany. The year 1968 is therefore synonymous with the politicization and mobilization of a generation of predominantly young intellectuals. After the failure of the revolts, they gradually distance themselves from their previous obsession with theories and ideological convictions. As a consequence of their basic anti-authoritarian philosophy and the anti-bourgeois lifestyle which was connected to it, however, they continued to determine the public image of the German intellectual for some time. As accomplished theoreticians, they were not interested in practical issues; they were obsessed by social utopias and thus necessarily critical of the existing status quo; they were indulgent and to some extent blind towards the weaknesses and dictatorial characteristics of socialist systems, but were hypercritical of Western policy, especially that of the USA in Vietnam; they were full of sympathy for the Third World, which was seen by them as a poor victim of Western imperialism.

Hans Magnus Enzensberger, one of Germany's leading and most brilliant intellectuals, was, at the time, a literary spokesman of the student revolts. He encouraged subversion against the Federal Republic and saw the Chinese Cultural Revolution as a model for Germany. He was frank about the role he played at this time in an interview with the newspaper *Die Zeit* on 20 January 1995. He saw in his own actions an example of the intellectual 'moral megalomania' which he himself later condemned. He commented as follows: 'Well, all that rhetoric was clearly a load of rubbish, that's not difficult to see. I do not deny that I was coming out with as much hot air as everybody else. But this does not alter the fact the political upheaval was necessary: it was only that which made this country – the Federal Republic of Germany – habitable for the first time.'

This is, of course, another example of the intellectual propensity for exaggeration.

It cannot be denied that the '68 generation has left an exceptional mark on the intellectual, cultural and even political life of the Federal Republic. The repercussions of 1968 are manifold. They include terrorism, the 'Citizen Initiatives' movement from which the Greens developed, the pacifism of the peace movement, in which leading left-wing intellectuals like Heinrich Böll and Walter Jens took an active part, and – from the politicians' side – the law banning the employment of radical teachers and civil servants, the *Radikalenerlaß*. Today, the '68 generation take the credit for transforming the Federal Republic into a genuine democracy worth living in; for liberating and loosening up German society, for expanding the education system and for enriching cultural life. This is all debatable, and it is possible to present an alternative version of what happened. Intellectual life at this time was characterized by levels of intolerance, ideologization and dogmatism that had been unheard of until then. It was a return to intellectual thought based on totalitarianism, romanticism and a criminal neglect of the value of truth. The balance of 1968 must therefore be characterized at least as unclear.

III. The Conservative Change of Course (from Schmidt to Kohl)

In 1982, the leader of the CDU, Helmut Kohl, came to power through a constructive vote of no confidence against the Social Democratic Chancellor Schmidt, a vote made possible by the FDP. This political change restored the bourgeois coalition of the Adenauer era and had also been preceded by an intellectual change of direction. This was an understandable and not unjustified reaction to the intellectual predominance of those on the Left who had begun to assert themselves after 1968. In a parallel development to what was going on in the United States and in England, it was this process that provided conservative thought with a bit more elbowroom and was supported by a large number of formerly liberal intellectuals against whom the critique of 1968 had been particularly vehement. Professors such as Richard Löwenthal, Thomas Nipperdey, Herman Lübbe and a number of others became spokesmen in the debate with left-wing theory and politics. Left-wing intellectuals did not disappear entirely from the intellectual stage, but their influence was noticeably reduced. This occurred parallel to political developments, since the conservative–liberal politics of Helmut Kohl and his coalition were now setting the agenda.

In the fifteen years between the Grand Coalition and the loss of power by the social-liberal coalition (1966–1982), intellectual and political life in the Federal Republic had indeed been both intense and eventful, with strong antagonistic and aggressive features. In the end, the conservative change of course was successful. It did not lead to the disappearance of radical left-wing thought, but did effectively tame it. It seemed that many of the intellectuals who, for so many years, had felt themselves unable to identify with the Federal Republic, were now making peace with it. Even under Helmut Kohl – someone of whom they did not think much – they were willing to come to terms with the conditions prevailing in Germany. For support of the fundamentals of its policies, the conservative government could at least rely on the functional intelligentsia in the state economic and social organizations. The 1968 dreams of a new republic were over; the free intellectuals devoted themselves once again to their aesthetic and private interests. Although they had little respect for politicians, they left politics to them. A number of prominent authors such as

Enzensberger, Martin Walser and Peter Schneider, who had become prominent through particularly vehement and highly political criticism of the system, now went their own ways and came to a more relaxed *modus vivendi* with the existing Federal Republic. The chasm between right and left became less deep.

The 1980s did not present intellectuals with any particular challenges. They were basically involved in their own affairs. How would they react when suddenly, out of the blue, the foundering of Soviet imperialism and the 'peaceful revolution' in the GDR would make the way clear for the end of Germany's forty-year division?

IV. German Intellectuals and Re-unification

Nobody – and that includes both politicians and intellectuals – was prepared for the fall of the Berlin Wall and the subsequent re-unification of Germany. The revolts of 1968 were the work of the students and intellectuals who had inspired them. The 'peaceful revolution' which swept the SED-state into oblivion came from below, from the people of the GDR. No German intellectuals, in either the Federal Republic or the GDR, took much part in it. GDR intellectuals of the calibre of Christa Wolf or Stefan Heym wanted a democratic, socialist GDR, but no unification with the Federal Republic; and many West German intellectuals were so afraid of Germany becoming a nationalistic world power again that they saw unification more as a danger than as anything to get excited about. Characteristic in this respect was the political stance taken by the Green Party, which unconditionally rejected re-unification, and also the hesitancy of the SPD, which at first saw more problems than opportunities in an eventual coming together of the two German states. The 1968 intellectuals were open in expressing their lack of interest in re-unification: the GDR seemed further away than the European countries to which they travelled so much – Florence was nearer than Dresden.

The West German attitude towards re-unification was more a question of generations than of politics. Those who had themselves experienced the division of Germany after the war and suffered under it since, pressed for what had at last become a possible and rapid solution to the German Question. Those born later did not share this emotional affinity. In as much as they were left-wing, they had little interest in seeing the spread of Western capitalism to East

Germany. If re-unification were inevitable, then it should at least occur through co-operation between the two German states and on the basis of a new, all-German constitution. This would be preferable to a simple accession of the GDR to the Federal Republic, which would seem more like a conquest of the one state by the other than a unification. Left-wing intellectuals warned of the colonization of the GDR by the FRG and criticized so-called 'Deutschmark Nationalism'. They had the misguided belief that – by drawing attention to some of the positive achievements of the GDR system – they would be able to bring about a better, more democratic, more socialist Federal Republic. This could not happen because the pressure in the GDR population to become part of the Federal Republic was too strong to resist, and because the GDR regime had been exposed as a fundamentally corrupt 'Stasi' system. This pressure from below meant that the GDR intellectuals had to forgo any influence on the process they might otherwise have enjoyed. Here, I do not just mean the very small groups of East German dissidents, but also those who collaborated with the system and those who were passively critical of it. Only very few GDR intellectuals now play a role in the intellectual and artistic life of the Federal Republic. The GDR writers, artists and intellectuals who had stabilized the old regime have withdrawn from public life in united Germany. They are having to deal with the damning indictment they receive from numerous colleagues who were forced by the system to leave for the West. Since the end of SED power, Wolf Biermann, the most prominent author expelled from the GDR, has continually condemned and denounced those colleagues who came to some kind of arrangement with the SED system.

German intellectuals in both East and West provided nothing more than accompanying music to the process of re-unification; they did not control the agenda. The decisive factors were first, the overwhelming majority of GDR citizens pressing for unification, and second, the political parties controlled from the West. These two factors helped Kohl's government, which had recognized, and was exploiting, the historical significance of what was happening. They helped the Federal Government attain the fundamental objective of German politics: the realization of the end of the division which had for so long seemed permanent. The intellectuals did, of course, concern themselves with these exciting historical events, and commented critically about them. They did not, however, significantly influence the form or execution of the re-unification process. They were observers, and politicians did not take much notice of them.

Intellectual controversies after the collapse of the GDR were predominantly internal affairs. Issues such as the ambiguous role played in the GDR system by the most significant female author in East Germany, Christa Wolf, or the collaboration between other authors and the Stasi were addressed. The song writer Wolf Biermann really had his day at this time, and spoke his mind accordingly. East German intellectuals also concerned themselves with the one-sided and strongly sympathetic judgements made by many West German publicists and academics on conditions in the GDR before the revolution and with the bizarre goings on in the West German authors' association, which the Stasi had even been able to influence. These were all internal debates that had no repercussions on the intellectual and political climate of the Federal Republic. East German intellectuals, unlike, for example, those in Poland, hardly contributed anything to the overthrow of the regime, and West German intellectuals hardly contributed anything to the intellectual orientation of the re-unification process.

V. German Intellectuals Today

Five years after the events of 1989, the internal debates on the role of intellectuals in the SED state and the attitude of West German intellectuals to the East German regime have more or less faded away. At the moment, the only debate is on how the still independent PEN club in the former GDR should be merged with the PEN centre in the Federal Republic. The issue at stake here is the political background of the GDR authors who were loyal to the regime. Those authors who were expelled from the GDR are justifiably protesting against the collective inclusion of the membership of the former GDR club in the German PEN club. This is not, however, an especially exciting issue, and nobody seems to be in a particular hurry to sort it out.

The violence of alienated and extreme right-wing youth against foreigners in both the former GDR (Hoyerswerda and Rostock) and the Federal Republic (Mölln and Solingen) was, however, a challenge for the intellectuals. Together with politicians they were decisive in their defence of the republic against violence and right-wing extremism. Candle-lit demonstrations were organized by young intellectuals throughout Germany to protest against violence and for a peaceful multicultural society. They were a manifestation of the willingness and determination of German intellectuals to protect the Federal Republic against a return to Weimar conditions.

The collapse of Soviet socialism and the exposure of the GDR as a pathetic political system which nobody – not even the PDS – would today dare to defend, have meant that the German intellectual Left – after its withdrawal from the ideologies and utopias of 1968 – has now been further weakened. Left-wing intellectuals have learnt to co-exist with the Federal Republic and devote themselves to their own individual intellectual interests, which they can pursue relatively unfettered. High levels of individualization and fragmentation – and a corresponding sense of de-politicization – are striking features of contemporary developments. At the October 1994 Federal elections, there was no significant support from intellectuals for the SPD's attempt to remove Kohl from power. The social democratic support networks set up by intellectuals that had been taken for granted by Willy Brandt were not provided for Scharping. It seemed as though left-wing and liberal intellectuals just did not care if Kohl stayed in power or not. They accepted his election victory without complaint.

The only phenomenon that occasionally seems to trouble left-wing intellectuals is the formation and effectiveness of a new intellectual right-wing movement. A group of formerly liberal and conservative intellectuals has become increasingly important in the debate with the dominant left on the legacy of 1968. They have drawn the battle lines with the New Left and shaken its cultural hegemony. They have attained more and more influence in the intellectual and political life of Germany.

With re-unification came the new problem of whether the re-establishment of a sovereign German nation state could lead to the emergence of a nationalistic right wing. There had always been a few right-wing intellectuals who had argued against the 'Westernization' of German society and politics and who had criticized the liberal and open characteristics of the German constitutional order. They did not, however, come anywhere near attaining the intellectual and political significance enjoyed by the right-wing intelligentsia of the Weimar Republic. They did not do so after re-unification, either; but it does seem that more intellectuals are moving from liberalism to conservatism today than before 1989. The Right does not, however, have any leading figures to guide it. This is why it orientates itself on the works of Carl Schmitt and other anti-liberal thinkers from the Weimar Republic. The *Historikerstreit* or 'debate of the historians' that took place before 1989 was an important example of this intellectual trend towards the Right. Those who argued in the debate against conservative attempts to relativize the crimes of the Nazis and to provide German history with a more positive sense of nationalism did, however, maintain the upper hand. How much longer will this be the case?

The conservative intelligentsia has never managed to form itself into an effective entity in the Federal Republic. Today, the right wing of the intellectual and political spectrum is, however, stronger than in earlier periods of German post-war history. This is not a change of direction towards a new form of nationalism and anti-liberalism because, unlike Weimar, the intellectual Centre is exceptionally strong. It was impressively represented between 1984 and 1994 in the person of the Federal President, Richard von Weizsäcker, and it seems that the new President, Herzog, is continuing along the same lines.

A characteristic of today's German intelligentsia is indeed that it contains this broad, heterogeneous centre which rejects all forms of extremism and is united in its defence of the basic principles of the democratic republic whenever these are seen to be in serious danger. Most German intellectuals have learnt from the experience of the Weimar Republic; they are aware that they have a public responsibility to maintain and secure liberal democracy. They subscribe less to the view that prevailed in Weimar times that intellect and power are diametrically opposed phenomena and that the free intellect is necessarily superior to power and must therefore lead it. Instead, they are aware that both aspects of the political – the intellectual and the practical – relate to and require each other. They have to engage in a productive and critical dialogue with one another.

Intellectual engagement in defence of the democratic constitutional order is of course dependent on the current condition of the polity. By making the point that intellectuals in the Federal Republic are rather quiet and reticent or that they are predominantly concerned with autonomous reflection, we show that the polity is in a good, or at least an acceptable, condition. This does not mean that intellectuals are dispensable, because politics are always changing, and perceptive, critical observation is necessary to stop things running out of control. This role of observers that the intellectuals should take up does, however, involve an obligation to intellectual honesty, an interest in the truth and an awareness of responsibility to the public at large. If the role is abused – and this happens again and again – then it is justifiable to speak of the intellectuals' having betrayed their mission. At the moment, this is not an issue in the Federal Republic. All in all, the role of intellectuals in the history of the Federal Republic has been a constructive and helpful one. There are many indications that this will remain the case in the near future.

Modern society needs the intellectuals, critics and original thinkers who do not just give power a free rein and who certainly do not let power deceive them. It also needs individualists who stand apart from mainstream opinion. It needs those with an ironic approach, who are able to perceive themselves and their environment with a sense of detachment. It needs sceptics who are distrustful of publicly propagated truths, but who, nevertheless, uphold the concept of truthfulness. It needs those with a creative imagination to whom things occur that the holders of power or the functional intelligentsia do not consider. It needs independent intellects that take responsibility for presenting the reality of societal conditions to the public at large. It needs those with the critical faculty necessary to consider these conditions in the context of their own values and objectives and then to question how they can be improved. Today in the Federal Republic we do enjoy conditions which – in terms of our history and by comparison with other countries in this world – must be described as rather good. However, even something that is relatively good still deserves and needs to be improved. If we are to avoid a return to something worse, something threatening and inhumane, then it is necessary to maintain and develop further, critically and with care, the positive things we have achieved. To do this, we need independent intellectuals.

Notes

1. Helmut Schelsky, *Die Arbeit tun die anderen. Klassenkampf und Priesterherrschaft der Intellektuellen*, Opladen 1975.
2. Kurt Sontheimer, *Das Elend unserer Intellektuellen. Linke Theorie in der Bundesrepublik Deutschland*, Hamburg 1967.
3. Kurt Sontheimer, *Die verunsicherte Republik*, Munich 1979, p.89.

THOMAS SIEVERTS

From the Task Force of Albert Speer for the Reconstruction of the Destroyed Cities to the International Building Exhibition Emscher Park – Cultures of Planning in Germany from 1943 to 1994[1]

I would like to begin with some autobiographical remarks. Having been born in 1934 and raised in Hamburg, I was 'traditionally' orientated towards the culture of the Anglo-Saxon world, and in addition to this 'natural' inclination by birth and family I underwent a lively 're-education in democracy' in the years after the war with the help of the 'British Centre' in Hamburg, with its library, lectures and exhibitions. Being passionately interested in architecture and town planning from the age of ten, I discovered during my school years and as a young student fascinating and revolutionary concepts in post-war Britain: e.g. Patrick Geddes's *Cities in Evolution*,[2] Ebenezer Howard's *Garden-Cities of Tomorrow*,[3] Abercrombie's, *Greater London Plan*,[4] and the *New Town Policy*.[5]

So it was quite natural for me as an architecture student to apply for a scholarship to study in England for two terms, and the *Studienstiftung des Deutschen Volkes* sent me to the School of Architecture and Civic Design in Liverpool, where I studied with great enjoyment for two terms in 1958, with many follow-up visits in my professional academic life in the form of student-exchanges, excursions and, last but not least, my five-year appointment as a special Professor at the University of Nottingham.

These lively connections cooled down on my side with Margaret Thatcher and the Falklands War. These events for me marked another Britain which had very little in common with the country and the people I loved. With this new visit now I shall try to find a new approach to this country so different from that of my student time, and I am very curious to analyse the shift from the socialist ideas of the 1950s to the current belief in the market as the main regulator of society.

If I try to discuss the 'cultures of town planning' in post-war Germany, I shall talk implicitly about the culture of local politics, and the culture of local politics again reflects attitudes of society to the past, to the present and to the future. Town planning is part of this cultural and political story, and though it may seem to be a rather technically specialized part of it, I hope to show you that it reflects intellectual and cultural developments. In my talk the cultures of town planning will serve as a paradigm. Therefore my main emphasis will be on the *procedures* of planning, because they reflect intellectual and cultural changes more clearly than the *results* of town planning – the built environment itself, which more often reflects economic and functional changes.

I.   The Period of Reconstruction from 1945 to 1960

As you know, nearly all German towns were bombed and more or less destroyed in the Second World War – the Royal Air Force was pretty successful at that game!

What you perhaps will not have quite as clearly in your mind, is the fact that Albert Speer, who was responsible for monumental Nazi plans to convert not only the centres of cities like Munich, Nuremberg and Berlin, but also many smaller towns into monuments of National Socialism, changed town planning policy radically after the lost battle of Stalingrad in 1943.

He founded the *Wiederaufbaustab* (task force for reconstruction) and called a number of well-known architects to prepare plans of reconstruction for the bombed cities, based on meticulous surveys of the grade of destruction in each city. Most of these architects were more technocrats than Nazis, many of them being pupils of famous architects of the 1920s.

This task force prepared comprehensive plans, which no longer demonstrated the conventional, uniform Nazi monumentalism, but ranged from conservative historical reconstruction to radical modern patterns of town planning. After the war these plans served as a basis for the repair and immediate reconstruction of cities until about 1949. This was the time of the reform of the German currency and the founding of the Federal Republic on the one hand and the GDR on the other. This first period, from Stalingrad to the currency reform, was a time in which the plans of the thirties were adapted to meet the demands of the *Wirtschaftswunder*, the so called 'economic miracle'.

But it was not only the plans of the *Wiederaufbaustab* which proved to be influential; some of the most prominent members of this task force were even more so.

Being excused from military service and therefore not having been prisoners of war, a number of architects from the *Wiederaufbaustab* could take over responsible jobs in the newly founded city administrations immediately after the end of the war. Best known are Rudolf Hillebrecht in Hanover and Friedrich Tamms in Dusseldorf, both of whom implemented the reconstruction of these cities most successfully until the 1970s.

Without analysing this phase between Stalingrad and the beginning of the 'economic miracle', it is hardly possible to understand the culture of town planning that lasted until about 1960, with the phase of the main reconstruction being from 1951 until 1957.

I called this period the 'time of the strong technocrats'. The obvious poverty of the time led to a political consensus in the aims of the reconstruction: politicians and population had great faith in the practical and theoretical expertise of the town planners. There was a strong belief in the merits of planning and its new techniques, as the future promised to be bright and economic progress was so obvious. So there was a great political and popular consensus when it came to reconstructing the towns and cities, and the necessary decisions were prepared and implemented in an astonishingly short time. It was a local society still based on personal authority, still structured in unquestioned hierarchies – Adenauer was the appropriate leader for this time.

The first public criticisms of the rapid reconstruction came in about the middle of the 1950s. These concentrated on the lost chances of radical modernization, especially the insufficient provision for the economic change from an industry-based to a service-oriented economy, and the inadequate provision of space for the increase in road traffic.

The city-areas were reconstructed mostly according to conservative historical city patterns, with some provision for new elements. These city centres were occupied by the fastest-growing sector of the economy – by service and retail-outlets. The quickly developing division of labour in a fast-growing national economy led to extending regional interlinkages, and this again led – reinforced by the growing wealth of the population – to rapidly expanding car ownership, which no longer found appropriate space for its vehicles.

If you look back, you get the impression that the war period really ended in Germany only with the period of reconstruction. The period from 1949 to about 1958 was a period of restoration, not only in the sense of reconstructing the buildings, but politically also. It was called a 'leaden time', and it was no wonder that a young architecture student like me should look to England as a Mecca for new and fresh political ideas.

With the fast-growing economy and its new demands for technical and social infrastructure, society was challenged to go beyond restoration and find new and adequate means in education, research, medical services, traffic and also town and regional planning. In this period of modernization, the towns had to take the main burden, but also to take the lead.

The local authorities of towns and cities in Germany are rooted in the famous reforms of Freiherr vom Stein, and are granted a strong position of self-government by our federal constitution, the *Grundgesetz*.

They faced up to these problems by trying to improve the situation intellectually and practically by initiating systematic inter-disciplinary studies to help town planners to understand the complex relationship between economic change, city growth, differentiation of land use patterns and demographic circumstances.

This produced a number of impressive studies which helped to establish town planning as an academic discipline; but there were insufficient legislative and economic tools to implement these proposals. The first national law on town planning, the *Bundes-baugesetz* of 1962, was a more or less conservative summary of existing planning tools and did not provide the necessary framework and perspectives for the solution of new and fast-growing problems.

II.   The Experiment in Planning Integrated City-Development: The Belief in Economic Growth, Systems Theory and Quantitative Computing Methods

At the beginning of the 1960s, the traffic problems caused by both an elaborate division of labour and growing real incomes, as well as the differentiated demands of social infrastructure, forced a re-evaluation of these new tools of planning and financing. The new methods and the power of planning for car traffic in the USA, based on the rapidly developing computer and strongly supported by the automobile industry, tended especially to destroy the traditional fabric of cities. This provoked serious criticism. The technocratic traffic engineer had to be 'tamed' by a more integrated system of planning that included not only the question of land use, but also the size of the public budget.

The deficits in public infrastructure, the discrepancies between growing suburbs and decaying city centres, as well as the uncoordinated and therefore conflicting work of different departments within the fast growing city administrations provided reason enough to search for a method of and an organization for integrated city development. A new method of planning seemed to be required, which not only co-ordinated the various planning departments, but also used budget planning as a powerful motor of well-balanced city development, especially as forecasts foresaw an enormous growth in cities.

Legislation followed in the form of special laws for the financing of communal traffic improvements and of urban renewal. In city government, new institutions of integrated planning and administration were implemented. Regional planning was organized in different forms, mainly in co-operation with local authorities. New programmes for financing urban renewal helped to realize ambitious planning programmes.

In this period between 1960 and 1975, and particularly between 1965 and 1972, the culture of planning was characterized by a new 'scientific', rational approach designed to create systematic planning procedures. Quantitative computing methods dominated the scene, with experiments in complex mathematical models to simulate city developments and real estate markets.

Alongside the traditional architect-planner, new practitioners entered the game: sociologists, economists and geographers. The first university courses in town planning were implemented. Predominant at that time was an optimistic but rather technocratic belief in the possibility of improving cities and society by the rational planning of space and economic growth.

This attitude of being potentially master of the world was not restricted to urban and regional planning, but also influenced national policies: new methods and laws to steer the national economy along 'Keynesian' lines, a national plan for the enormous extension of universities and special laws for regulating urban expansion were significant for the political spirit of the age, still dominated by a powerful technocracy, which was later criticized by the student radicals in the late 1960s.

The student revolt in 1968 showed an ambivalent attitude to this spirit. On the one hand, the students discovered the political character of every kind of planning and its unequal distribution of benefits and burdens in society, and therefore they demanded more democracy in planning and more participation by the population.

On the other hand, the student revolt of 1968 shared the belief of its enemies, the 'establishment', in the power of scientifically based rational arguments and in the chances of improving the world by rational planning, making use of industrialization and the benefits of strong, if more justly distributed, economic growth.

Ecological arguments were nearly non-existent in the thought and arguments of 1968. This 'revolt' was far removed from the ecological movements that appeared a few years later. But even so, the student revolt changed the climate of German society drastically; it marked the definite end of the Adenauer era.

The experiences with the new methods of integrated planning and the results of the new organizational units of integrated administration were disappointing. Soon new insights into both the complexity of the problems and the changed socio-economic conditions led to a much more modest attitude. The new demand for popular participation and more direct democracy added to the difficulties in handling the new techniques of town planning.

The main reasons for the changes in attitudes were the following:

•   *Too much complexity*. The demand to integrate nearly every aspect of relevance into planning led to such complex planning documents that the contents could not be translated into practical politics and administration.

- *Too little precision.* When asked for practical and implementable solutions for an actual problem, the characteristically general attitude of the integrationist could not compete with the precision of the specialist. Therefore the integrationists were open to the charge that they were not 'serious'.
- *The improvement of planning tools for certain policies which had special political priority.* Traffic especially, and also the other competing fields of politics – housing, recreational space, etc., developed their own technical methods and bureaucratic power in confrontation with integrated planning, with its aim of harmonizing the different conflicting interests on a general level.
- *Lack of public response.* The unavoidably high level of abstraction in integrated planning made it nearly impossible to arouse public interest, especially as it belonged to the prophylactic nature of this method to deal with problems that were expected in the future and were thus not yet evident to the public.
- *Difficulties in adapting the planning documents to new demands.* Complexity allows only slow adaptation and needs a lot of input, so it can be implemented only from time to time. Therefore actual political decisions were taken outside the framework of this kind of planning, which therefore deteriorated into a kind of 'bookkeeping' for decisions taken for other reasons.
- *Unsteady public financing.* Integrated planning needs more or less steady public financing. With the growing integration of national economies into a world economy, public budgets were less under national control. City development became more and more dependent on the ups and downs of an internationally structured economy.
- *Unsteady economic growth.* Development planning was based on the concept of steady economic growth. The critique of this concept, based on ecological reasoning, led to a fundamental ideological questioning of the integrationalists' attitude.
- *The failure in forecasting.* The paradigm of scientific thinking, that it is in principle possible to improve techniques of social and economic forecasting, and the scientific and political belief in trends and steady growth, was destroyed both by chaos theory, with proves that it is theoretically impossible to forecast the behaviour of complex systems, and by the practical experience of the 'oil crisis' in 1974, which undermined the very basis of economic forecasting, the price-structure of the energy market.

- *The lack of sensitivity to ecological problems.* Ecology did not have an adequate role in the integrated planning of that time. Ecological crises, and a growing public sensitivity to the importance of ecological stability, challenged the theory of economic growth in a most fundamental way.

The intellectual fathers of the idea of integrated development planning rapidly discovered these weaknesses and tried to 'rescue' their philosophy by reducing its complexity, but they were not successful.

In the 1970s, both severe economic problems and criticism from the right wing of the political spectrum of the political philosophy of state intervention led to demands for the 'deregulation' of administrative influence and power and to a monetarist policy, which aimed at lowering the level of taxation.

Both policies 'killed off' the method of integrative development-planning, as they simultaneously attacked its ideological, method-ological and financial foundations.

Of course, this rather drastic change from belief in strong state intervention to belief in the power of self-regulation of the market again reflected a worldwide change in political climate at the time, and town planning did not escape the tide of change.

The philosophy of integrated planning of city development was radically questioned, not only from the political 'right' but also from the 'left'. The ecological movement challenged the ideological base of economic growth by constituting its own model of ecological balance.

Challenged from the left and the right, with unfulfilled dreams and in a period of economic slump, town planning escaped into a new historicism.

III.   From the New Historicism of Conservative Urban Renewal to the Present Situation

The radical change in the public mood was marked by the 'year of cultural heritage' in 1975.

The modern, progress-oriented positivism, with its belief in systems theory and quantitative methods, quickly changed into a 'postmodern' backward-looking attitude. Reactionary, non-materialistic and historical values were combined with 'progressive' ecological reformist attitudes in a most peculiar way, which I think is typical of German political culture.

In no other country in Europe is the 'Green' party so strong as it is in Germany, and in this party conservative values of protecting natural and cultural assets mix with 'progressive' values of strong state intervention, especially to safeguard the ecological balance. So values of the political 'right' based on the German romanticism of the nineteenth century are sometimes in conflict with a new form of ecological socialism.

From the 'year of cultural heritage' in 1975 to the opening of the 'Iron Curtain' in 1989 the culture of city planning was dominated by small-scale urban renewal and urban design, improving the public space and caring for public monuments. The participation of the inhabitants was developed into an integral part of civic culture in some towns and cities. This policy was generally most successful in West Germany and the deterioration of the inner city, which is typical for towns in the USA, was avoided. The policy also led to the consolidation of the inner city; love and care went exclusively to the centre, and the periphery was neglected completely. This might be symbolic of Germany's political culture, which did not care enough for its 'fringe-problems' in other fields either.

In the terms of planning theory, this period could be described as 'incrementalist planning': it involved many small steps, loosely co-ordinated by the informal framework of a 'masterplan'.

It was a period of rediscovered sensitivity to the non-materialistic values of townscape, of the values of atmosphere, history and special socio-economic milieux.

This sensitivity to the values of the existing historic cities and the continuous effort needed to re-evaluate them for present purposes is one of the great assets of the culture of civic design in post-war Germany. Of course it also marks a questionable attitude to restoration, which is especially predominant in East Germany now.

Since the opening up of Eastern Europe in 1989, the scene has changed drastically once more. Immigration, socio-economic changes and socio-demographic transformations have led to an enormous demand for new dwellings, and the necessary urban renewal in East Germany – both in the old centres and in the industrial areas, as well as in the monotonous prefab housing-areas – takes up a considerable part of the national income and leads to severe political stress.

Again the existing planning procedures were not adequate for the new problems. Public budgets were diminishing, ecology-movements were fighting urban expansion, and, last but not least, the political-administrative situation in the former GDR did not allow for the transfer of the most differentiated planning procedures of West Germany to East Germany. Even in West Germany, the elaborate planning procedures proved more and more detrimental to the solution of new problems.

New and simpler forms of planning procedures therefore were introduced in East Germany, and soon transferred to West Germany as well. The re-unification of Germany, and the drain on the budgets of local authorities caused by huge capital transfers from West to East, speeded up a far-reaching reform of public administration. Former public services are now being privatized, and many public investments are being made in the form of public-private partnerships, with the goal of a 'lean administration' on the analogy of 'lean management'. In this field the experiences in Britain from the Thatcher era to the present day served as important examples.

But it was not only the raising of the Iron Curtain that led to a reform of planning procedures; independent developments in economy and society also forced a consideration of new forms of administration:

- The German economy underwent a quick and painful transformation from a 'Fordist' industry of mass-production to post-Fordist structures of client-tailored services.
- Immigration and social segregation along ethno-cultural lines confronted politicians and city planners with problems unknown in Germany before.
- The ecology movement had grown into a powerful and independent political force.
- Last but not least, the higher level of education had improved the skills of political articulation and self-organization inside the public protest movements.

The new nature of problems – for example the high level of structurally-based unemployment, the endangered balance of ecology, and the stresses of a multicultural society – did not allow authorities to follow the old conventional paths of town planning.

If you look for a common denominator in the new tasks, you find terms like 'innovation' and 'motivation'. Obviously planning cannot even theoretically offer solutions for some of the most important problems any more; but it may contribute to an innovative climate and to a systematic presentation of the conflicting issues to the public, which then might find consensus in a complex process of a public discussion, moderated by planners.

The lack of a general socio-economic theory forces one down a path of 'trial and error', and to develop solutions which are open for revision and change. This new modesty is not only valid for town planning, but for local authority politics in general, for example in the fields of education, health care and housing. It reflects a new relationship between people and the state, the state not being any longer the god-like authority, but becoming a kind of service agency for the people.

IV. 'Perspective Incrementalism' as an Answer to the Changed Situation

Our society has obviously reached a degree of complexity which can no longer be controlled using the traditional tools of planning and the 'planning commands' of the state. Without the active involvement and productively motivated interest of the people, planning remains sterile in a peculiar way. The international competitiveness of society quite obviously depends on the quality, motivation and mobility of its 'human capital'.

After having analysed the different cultures of planning over the last 50 years, and bearing in mind the changed historical and socio-economic situation, we have tried to formulate a new approach. It integrates sensitivity to ecological aspects and historical values typical of the recent past, and uses the still existing administrative and financial heritage from the period of integrated planning in the form of specialized programmes and planning laws. We have given to this attitude the somewhat pompous name of 'perspective incrementalism'.

In planning theory, 'incrementalism' was once, in the period of the integrated planning approach, a kind of 'swear word', used to denounce the world of 'muddling through' in planning.

At present a new kind of 'enlightened muddling through' seems not such a bad approach, and the attribute 'perspective' simply means to gear the large number of small steps of single planning decisions into a general direction. In other words: 'Perspective incrementalism' tries to combine the practicability of 'muddling through' with the ambitions of the integrative approach!

The main features of 'perspective incrementalism' are:

1. Planning goals remain on a general, principled level and are orientated around general values in society. This convinces the public and makes it easier to find a political consensus.
2. The true realization of the generally defined goals and principles will be tested with actual 'real-life projects'. The loyalty generated by general political goals that have been tested in practice contributes to the credibility of planning.
3. Concrete but also complex projects carry the message of planning, instead of elaborate general planning programmes, which are always more or less abstract. The tools of planning and financing are tailored to these projects. The programme will evolve by connecting complex projects, not the other way round.
4. Easily comprehensible phases are introduced instead of long-term programmes with an open perspective. This principle makes it easier for the public to understand the goals of planning and for the political and administrative institutions to revise their goals from time to time.
5. Planning efforts are concentrated in time and space to 'areas of action', instead of trying to create a perfect system of planning for all scales and each territorial unit that also covers large areas without any acute problems.
6. The integration of planning tools instead of programmes enables one to implement complex projects that do not fit into specialized programmes. The different programmes are separated into different sections and connected again to fit into the structure of a complex project.
7. Economic instead of legal intervention will be more successful, especially in Germany, with its possibly over-elaborate legal system and court machinery.

With the help of these rather pragmatic principles we try to find a balance of 'muddling through' and developing a new culture of planning, which is realized in the International Building Exhibition *Emscher Park*. Building Exhibitions have served in Germany, for nearly 100 years now, to spread and accelerate changes in ideas by experimenting with new forms of planning procedures.

V. An Example: The International Building Exhibition at *Emscher Park*

The philosophy of 'perspective incrementalism' dominates the International Building exhibition at *Emscher Park*. This 'workshop for the renewal of old industrial areas' belongs to the level of what we call 'intermediate organizations'. Limited to two periods of five years each, this organization has neither legal power nor investment capital of its own. Its influence is indirect: as a 'dependency' of the *Land* of North-Rhine-Westphalia it influences the priorities of public subsidies by improving projects to very high standards.

The IBA Emscher Park organizes competitions and workshops; it gives organizational help and expertise, as well as advice, to local authorities and, last but not least, it fixes quality standards for the implementation of projects.

This continuous work of persuasion and convincing, of discussion and qualification, helps to mobilize the regional intellectual resources and initiatives, which have lost momentum and power with the decline of the coal and steel industries and have not yet quite recovered: the Ruhr area was formerly dominated by the 'dinosaurs' of the 'Ruhr coal industry'. Small and middle-sized firms and service industries are far below the national average, and need an intellectual stimulus.

The experiences which can be drawn from this kind of indirect planning by persuasion, competition of ideas and evaluation are manifold. They show some parallels to modern management: the combination of different tools of planning and financing and the close co-operation of different departments of public administration and private firms demand integrated work for each complex project. This means a kind of 'revolution' in bureaucracy, which normally works like a conveyor-belt, each file being handled by each department along the 'conveyor-belt' of time, with each applying its own independent standards. In this new situation they have to work simultaneously in time and space, sitting around one 'common table', exchanging arguments, without relying on the classic norms and hierarchies of administration.

In this simultaneous work, administrative processes and standards are interpreted in a creative way. Some old and cynical administrators find new pride and energy by contributing to the realization of a complex and beautiful project. The imagination of the 'software' of innovative processes becomes as important as the imagination of the 'hardware' of innovative projects, through the intelligent combination of different sources of financing and tools of administration, through bringing together the right people and through mobilizing the public.

Using this approach, this 'workshop for the renewal of old industrial areas' tries to create a special innovative intellectual milieu and environment for each project. Small projects are trusted to the normal routine of existing administration and private firms. For larger, more complex projects, special types of development corporation are organized, mostly in the form of public–private partnerships.

This culture of planning works on three different levels:

1. on the pragmatic level of the 'hardware' of the projects itself by the satisfaction of the actual user;
2. on the symbolic level of the general message of the projects distributed by the different media; and
3. on the educational level of the awareness of the many active people involved in planning and realization.

The IBA *Emscher Park* again reflects the actual scene of political discussion and administrative reform of local authorities. They use their strong position in public life and their power, given by the constitution, to experiment with different reforms. By organizing public administration and budgeting according to the principles of 'lean management' from private business, by privatizing even classic departments of public administration such as the department of public works and by trying to find forms of social services, for old people for example, that no longer concentrate on old people's homes but are integrated into the daily life of the neighbourhood in a decentralized pattern.

Local authorities in Germany share these experiments with other countries in Europe, and again in this field Britain has many ideas and experiences to offer to Europe, as it has started the business of 'deregulation' earlier than other states. It is this new role of the state which interests me most in Britain these days.

The special historical path of Germany since the Second World War not only in the field of town planning but also in local authority government now becomes part of a European culture of planning, whose future is still open.

Will it become more or less unified by common administrative procedures, dictated by Brussels, or will it develop further the lively variety and differences embedded in the many different cultures of its members?

Will Europe be able to defend its great historical tradition in caring for those social, aesthetic and ecological qualities of its towns and cities that cannot be valued in terms of money?

Or will Europe leave its towns and cities more or less exclusively to the market economy? In this process they would become more and more Americanized, and lose their cultural traditions for ever.

I hope very much that Britain, together with Germany and the other members of the European Community, will defend and develop further its great tradition in this field, even against the commercial spirit of Brussels!

Notes

1. This chapter is based on an article, written together with Karl Ganser, 'Vom Aufbaustab Speer bis zur Internationalen Bauausstellung Emscher Park und darüber hinaus – Planungskulturen in der Bundesrepublik Deutschland', *Dokumente und Informationen Schweizer Planer*, 115, October 1993, pp. 31–7.
2. Patrick Geddes, *Cities in Evolution*, London 1968.
3. Ebenezer Howard, *Garden Cities of Tomorrow*, London 1951, p. 168.
4. Patrick Abercrombie, *Greater London Plan 1944*, London 1945, p. 220.
5. Patrick Abercrombie, *New Town Policy*, London 1946.

WOLFGANG WELSCH

Modernity and Postmodernity in Post-War Germany (1945-1995)

Two conceptual remarks to begin with. First: 'modernity' is less a concept than a term – and a complex one at that. It comprises at least four dimensions: economic–technical, social, political, and cultural. And there is neither a neat unity nor a necessary congruence between these different aspects. In most cases, modern societies exhibit considerable disparities and even contradictions between these dimensions. The unity of what we call 'modernity' is not due to an essential core common to all these dimensions, but to partial overlaps and interrelations – to family resemblance – between them. Hence, the proper way to speak about modernity is to look at these dimensions separately.[1]

Secondly: I suggest distinguishing between two levels of the usage of the term 'modernity': an operative and a reflective one. People use the term operatively in order to promote or to criticize modernization, or to describe their attitudes with respect to modernity. But even if nobody in a given society uses the term, it might be appropriate to describe this society as a modern one. One can very well be modern without ever having heard the term – just as Molière's Monsieur Jourdain one day gladly discovered that he had been speaking prose for years without knowing it.[2]

I. Modernity

1. Economic and Technical Modernity in the Early Federal Republic

In the early Federal Republic 'modern' soon became an operative term. In October 1953, for example, Chancellor Adenauer, in his Declaration of Government, pronounced it 'the most important goal of our policy in economics to modernize industrial plants'. 'Renewal and modernization, rationalization, education of highly qualified skilled workers are urgent.'

But there are two restrictions in this operative usage of 'modern' and 'modernization'; they are too limited and too imprecise. First, the terms refer only to the economic–technical sphere. They are synonymous with economic and technical progress, implying both rationalization and innovation, but not – at least not in any conscious or explicit way – social, political or cultural modernization. They designate merely economic and technical advance. This may implicitly be understood as the main condition for advance in other spheres too, but the connection is never made explicit. Secondly, the term 'modern' is not the proper term with which to advocate economic–technical progress or of the attractiveness of this advance. There is no need to use it when advocating such development. Other appealing terms such as 'prosperity', 'progress', 'economic growth' or simply 'future' serve the same purpose. The basic feature is that of a widespread admiration of technology and of a belief in technical progress. This is why the term 'modern' is less often used than one might expect. It is not a key term for the period. But economic and technical progress is its key issue.

So the early Federal Republic clearly wanted to be modern and affirmed modernity – but only in the sense of economic and technical modernity, and without putting particular emphasis on the notion of 'modernity' itself.

2. 'Modernity' in the Middle Years of the Federal Republic

Only twenty years later, 'modern' and 'modernity' became more meaningful (and at the same time controversial) terms. In the 1969 election campaign, the Social Democratic Party proclaimed: 'We will create the modern Germany',[3] whereas the CDU slogan was: 'It is the Chancellor who counts.'[4] In this SPD slogan, 'modern

Germany' clearly had a broader meaning than the modernity Adenauer had advocated in 1953, when he spoke only of the modernization of industrial plant, or in 1961, when, again speaking only of a case of technical modernization, he announced in another statement of policy by the government that there would be 'the rationalization and modernization' of the Federal Railways. In 1969 the appeal for modernity implied not only economic and technical progress, which nevertheless, with Karl Schiller as designated Minister of Economics, remained prominent, but also social progress, for example by making factory committees obligatory, and considerable changes in foreign policy, especially in the new *Ostpolitik*.

Nevertheless the term 'modern' remained imprecise. In a rather diffuse manner it implied 'change' and 'progress' in general. It somehow corresponded to the allusions to progress in the title of the SPD weekly *Vorwärts* (Forward). The direction of this 'forward' was in no way determined by any well-defined or normative content in the term 'modern'. 'Modern' was just an obviously appealing term – perhaps especially after the student revolt of 1968 and because of the diffuse and broad connotations it could carry.

3.   The Modernity of Modern Art

In another sphere however, the term 'modern' had a very clear meaning from the beginning: in the sphere of the arts.

a. The Turn to Modern Art in the Early Federal Republic   The early Federal Republic took a surprising turn towards the appreciation of modern art. The Germans overcame the National Socialist condemnation of modern art and redefined themselves – at least in as far as they were interested in art – as modern by promoting modern art. The series of *Documenta* exhibitions, which began in 1955 and soon became the most important exhibition of contemporary art worldwide, is a clear indication of this. Werner Haftmann, the chief commissioner of the first *Documenta*, made Kandinsky's proclamation of Great Realism and Great Abstractionism the basis of the new Germany's understanding of modern art.[5] This pattern allowed both the integration of condemned German Expressionism and the introduction of European and American Abstractionism. The *Westkunst* (Western Art) exhibition in Cologne in 1981 was a logical consequence of this turn to modern, Western art. However, by 1981 this concept had already become too narrow, as some critics pointed out. It needed to be supplemented by considering Eastern German and Eastern European art too. Art was once again a mirror of developments to come.

In the early Federal Republic, the artistic sphere was the only one where the term 'modern' had a strong and clear meaning. First of all it designated the breakdown of traditional representation and the shift to non-representational, autonomous works of art, with abstract art being the most outstanding example of this change.[6] Secondly, and as a consequence of this shift beyond representation, modern art has become experimental and innovative in principle, and proceeds in a possibly never-ending series of different trends and -isms. Its basic principle of breaking with tradition remains the enduring impulse which is acted out through continual change and innovation.

Because of this formal law of change, progress and innovation, the artistic definition of 'modern' could easily apply to other spheres. Owing to its formal avant-garde character, it could also unconsciously support the pursuit of economic and technical modernization, with neither art nor technology defining a goal to aim for, but just advocating going forward, affirming progress as such.

Modern art was – in short – the very archetype of modernity during these years.[7] When intellectuals asked themselves what 'modern' meant to them, the answer was constantly given by pointing to the paradigm of modern art. Even if the stomach was rumbling, eyes lit up in the face of modern art, as Erhart Kästner put it.[8]

A clear sign of the paradigmatic character of modern art is the fact that encyclopaedias in the Federal Republic such as the *Große Brockhaus* had very extensive entries on modern painting and sculpture from the beginning, and later also on modern graphic arts, modern music, architecture and dance; these entries covered one to four pages. But the entries on 'modern' and 'modernity' in general were very small – only two to five lines, and there was no entry at all on *die Moderne* (the Modern Age) until 1991.

b. The Controversy about Modern Art Whenever there was a struggle about modernity in the early Federal Republic, it was about modern art – this being, as I have tried to point out, the exemplary sphere of modernity, which in addition provided a strong point of identification for those who really wanted to break with Nazism. The most prominent rejection of modern art came from Hans Sedlmayr (an art historian, who during the Nazi period had been an outspoken supporter of the movement). In 1948, in his book *Der Verlust der Mitte* ('The Lost Centre'), he renewed the Nazi attack on modern art from an Occidental Catholic perspective. Modern art, Sedlmayr said, destroys the integrity of man, and this is a consequence of the misleading modern principle of autonomy and of mankind's turn to atheism. The sole remedy should therefore consist in a return to the acknowledgement of the real Centre, of God. The book was a great success, because Sedlmayr's view could be shared both by conservatives, who at that time advocated a return to what they called the Occidental or Christian tradition, whose values, so they argued, represented the only effective protection against Nazism, and by those who were still sympathetic towards the Nazi ideology. Sedlmayr's attack on modern art provided an ideal focus for anti-modern tendencies of all kinds.[9]

So, with regard to modern art, a polarization took place in the early Federal Republic between modernists on the one hand – and by 'modernists' I mean people who advocated modern art and who in doing so affirmed modernity in general – and anti-modernists and modernity-sceptics of different kinds on the other, who opposed modern art and thereby expressed their scepticism about other facets of modernity, too.

To summarize these considerations. There was no debate about modernity as such in the early Federal Republic. But one took place in an indirect form: in the guise of a debate about modern art. Much more than art was at stake in this debate. By defining their attitude towards modern art, people also defined their relationship towards key issues of modernity, such as democracy, social development, re-education, Westernization, etc.

4. The Attitude to Economic and Technical Modernity and to Modern Art in the Early German Democratic Republic

On the terminological level there were almost no differences between the two Germanies at this time. The terms 'modern' and 'modernization' were of very limited operative use in the German Democratic Republic too. They indicated solely economic and technical measures to increase efficiency and in most cases pertained only to the improvement of machines.

Yet there was a slight as well as a major difference. In encyclopaedias, the term 'modern age' – which was omitted in Western encyclopaedias until 1991 – occurred as early as in 1964, but only in a negative sense, and this points to the major difference. What the terms 'Modern Age' and 'modernism' designate, is decadent Western art. Three main objections were raised. The break with artistic tradition and experience, which is constitutive of modernism, undermines the common comprehensibility of art, this now being understandable only for an élite. It furthermore engenders a trend to pseudo-innovation and pseudo-originality which corresponds all too well to the demands of a capitalist market. And finally, it eliminates the human meaning and importance of art, this being replaced by mere formalism; autonomy in art is the wrong perspective, social commitment would be the right one. In short, Western modernism reinstitutes the standards and contradictions of bourgeois Western culture and capitalism. Hence Socialist Realism and modernism are incompatible.[10]

So modern art is again – as we saw already within the Western debate – a test case for the attitude to modernity in general. But this time the result is not a polarization, but a rejection. In the German Democratic Republic 'modernity' and 'modernism' were clearly negative notions.

The comparison between the two German states thus far can be summarized as follows. There is an obvious congruence between Federal Republic and Democratic Republic with respect to the affirmation of technical modernization, but there is a clear contrast with respect to modernity and modernization in the field of the arts and of social and political culture in general, modernity being affirmed, at least in principle – however reservedly – by the main groups in the Federal Republic, but rejected in the Democratic Republic. The only correspondence is between conservative and reactionary groups in the Federal Republic and the official ideology in the Democratic Republic – but for obviously different reasons.

5. Social and Political Modernity

a. General Remarks   Now I want to consider the aspects of social and political modernity in the two German states. As the operative use of the terms 'modern' and 'modernity' was limited to economic and technical modernization and to modern art, in order to discuss these further aspects, we now have to move from the operative to the reflective level. In what ways were the two German states to be called 'modern'?

The reflective use of 'modernity' was introduced by Western social and political theory during the 1950s. Daniel Lerner's book *The Passing of Traditional Society: Modernizing the Middle East* of 1958 was very influential and significant: modernization was understood to contrast with being traditional, and the concept was originally used to analyse the social and political development in underdeveloped countries. But later, in the 1960s, it also served to analyse the evolution of Western industrial societies. American society was the model, and the term modernity covered both industrialization and democratization, including reflection on the social preconditions for, and the consequences of, this development.

This concept of modernity was applied to Germany for the first time in 1965 by Ralf Dahrendorf, in his book on *Society and Democracy in Germany*. I will mostly follow his analysis, with only one major modification, which is a consequence of the fact that I shall also try to cover the last thirty years.

b. The Federal Republic   The Federal Republic became a very modern country in almost every sense. Firstly, equal citizenship rights were guaranteed beyond doubt. Secondly, social modernity too developed considerably: equal opportunities were largely guaranteed; inherited privilege was replaced by acquired social standing (consider for example, that even the CDU, in the 1965 election campaign commended itself as the appropriate party for Germany's 'modern classless society'); and German élites are functional élites, in contrast for instance to the educational élites in France or England. Thirdly, 'the institutional recognition of social conflict in all sectors of society' has increased,[11] including reasonably successful management of these conflicts. Finally, even the dark side of modernity in the Federal Republic, its restriction by a widespread 'attitude of traditionalism',[12] which Dahrendorf pointed to in 1965, isn't all that dark and dominant any more. This attitude, which was represented by the CDU and by traditional factions in the SPD, and is still represented by the CSU – an attitude which preserved outdated methods of working in agriculture or steelworks, prevented people from turning to job-mobility and altogether hindered the road to modernity – has considerably diminished, especially since the 1968 student revolt with its attack on open and hidden national socialist strands within the leadership and the mentality of the early Federal Republic. Today's problems are in any case different and derive no longer from mere traditionalism.[13]

So the Federal Republic soon gave rise to a society of notable modernity, a modernity which has since increased still further.[14] Precisely because it had to catch up with its neighbours, its modernization was particularly strident. From the outside, the society of the 'economic miracle' in the 1960s was already perceived as being 'amazingly and dangerously modern'.[15] I suppose similar assessments were made in 1990.

c. The German Democratic Republic   The Democratic Republic was in one sense very modern. Dahrendorf even called it 'the first modern society on German soil'.[16] Institutionalizing social equality – by destroying all kinds of inherited privilege, by guaranteeing the right to employment, etc. – it provided all the social preconditions for the role of the citizen, people participating in the social and political processes almost entirely as public beings.[17] But the German Democratic Republic provided only the social preconditions for, not the formal rights of citizenship. There was *de facto* 'no universal, equal, free, and secret suffrage, no liberty of the person and of political activity, no equality before the law'.[18] So, paradoxically, East German society was 'a society that would enable its members to make effective use of these liberties, if only they had them'.[19] Clearly being modern on the social level, it was not modern at all on the political level.[20] And this disparity could, of course, in turn influence social conditions. Once people had had an open conflict with the state, they were no longer socially equal.

Compared to the Weimar Republic, the German Democratic Republic constituted a reversal, for 'in the Weimar Republic the role of the citizen was formally guaranteed to all, whereas this offer was undermined by the absence of the social preconditions for its realization'.[21] And compared with National Socialism – whose social revolution destroyed 'the traditional basis of German society in family and religion and all other spheres', and thus represented an unintended but nevertheless very effective 'push toward modernity',[22] the German Democratic Republic shared both the decisive break with tradition and the lack of citizenship rights. Finally, comparing the German Democratic Republic to the Federal Republic, it was – at least in principle – more advanced on the social, but drastically behind on the political level of modernity. Hence, theoretically speaking, a combination of the German Democratic Republic's social and the Federal Republic's political culture might have stood a chance in 1990. But nothing of the sort happened, as we all know. Was what happened instead a step into postmodernity?

II. Postmodernity

1. An Outline of the History of the Term 'Postmodern' and the Concept of Postmodernity

Postmodernity is a reflective concept. At a certain point in time, some scholars started describing the most developed societies as postmodern instead of modern. Let me first give a brief sketch of the rise of the term.

a. Sociology In sociology, the term was first introduced in 1968 by Amitai Etzioni, in his sketch of the 'active society' of the 'postmodern age',[23] which he characterized as 'a society responsive to its changing membership, one engaged in an intensive and perpetual self-transformation'.[24] In 1979 Jean-François Lyotard described the plurality of this postmodern society as follows: 'The social bond is linguistic, but is not woven with a single thread. It is a fabric formed by the intersection of [. . .] an indeterminate number of language games obeying different rules.[25] [. . .] nobody speaks all of those languages; they have no universal metalanguage [. . .] That is what the postmodern world is all about.'[26]

b. Literature But sociology was not the first sphere in which the term 'postmodern' came into use. This was more the case in the arts, especially with respect to literature.[27] Incidentally, the term 'postmodern' appeared for the very first time as early as in 1870, when the English painter John Watkins Chapman – not finding successors at that time – declared the next, post-impressionist step in painting to be postmodern. However the general debate about postmodernism, which continues up to the present day, began in 1959, when Irving Howe – soon followed by Harry Levin – characterized contemporary literature as weaker and less innovative than the great literature of modernity – the literature of Yeats, Eliot, Pound and Joyce.[28] Shortly thereafter, in the mid-1960s, critics like Leslie Fiedler and Susan Sontag developed a positive understanding of this new, postmodern type of literature, which for them was represented by Boris Vian, John Barth, Leonard Cohen or Norman Mailer. Fiedler – especially in his essay *Cross the Border – Close the Gap* of 1969 – praised the links between élitist and popular culture forged by these writers.[29] The postmodern artist is, according to Fiedler, a multilingual *Double Agent*,[30] 'equally at home in the world of technology and the realm of wonder'.[31] Postmodern literature is semantically and socially double-coded; it engenders a combination both of reality and fiction and of élitist and popular taste.

c. Architecture   The next step was made by Charles Jencks, who transferred Fiedler's concept to architecture – and he was so successful in doing so that to this day many people think postmodernism was originally an architectural movement. But apart from several isolated previous occurrences of the term – I have already mentioned Chapman and could add Rudolf Pannwitz, Federico de Oníz, Arnold Toynbee, D.C. Somervell, Joseph Hudnut and Peter F. Drucker – it was the American debate about literature from 1959 onwards, and not Jencks's book *The Language of Post-Modern Architecture* of 1977, which formed the beginning of the debate; Jencks just translated Fiedler's literary denominations into architectural ones. With Jencks, Fiedler's literary *Double Agent* became an architectural master of 'dual coding',[32] and the very goal of postmodern architecture came to consist in closing the gap and crossing the border between élitist and popular taste by means of steel girders plus columns.

2.   *The Origins of the Debate on Modernity and Postmodernity in the Federal Republic*

In 1968, Leslie Fiedler gave a talk in the Federal Republic on *The Case of Post-Modernism*, which was followed by a debate in the weekly *Christ und Welt* (Christian and World), in which prominent intellectuals and writers like Helmut Heissenbüttel, Martin Walser, Hans Egon Holthusen and Rolf-Dieter Brinkmann participated. The key event, however, was the discussion about the *Neue Staatsgalerie* (New State Gallery) in Stuttgart in the late 1970s and early 1980s. The focus of the competition – begun in 1977 – was between the German modernist Günter Behnisch, who came up with another version of the modernist glass container, and the British late- or post-modernist architect Charles Stirling, who proposed a building which would combine different styles and patterns – an architecture of 'complexity and contradiction', such as Robert Venturi, a avant-coureur of postmodern architecture, had advocated in 1966.[33] Stirling won the competition, but even after he had finished the museum in 1984 the discussion continued. Modern architecture – firmly established in the Federal Republic – was apparently about to lose its monopoly, and this was not just a question of the loss of a fiefdom, but of cultural orientation. Stirling's success seemed to signal a break with modernity.

In the meantime the issue of postmodernism had become a philosophical one too, as a result of Jean-François Lyotard's programmatic essay *The Postmodern Condition*, published in 1979. In the Federal Republic, the counter-attack by Jürgen Habermas in his Adorno Prize speech *Modernity – an unfinished project* in 1980 contributed to establishing postmodernism as a philosophical issue.[34]

In the course of this discussion not only 'postmodernity', but finally also 'modernity' acquired a precise meaning. This may have been desirable and called for in the case of postmodernity, as this term had thus far been vague and imprecise, although *à la mode*; but in the case of modernity it might seem surprising. Yet it isn't. Remember the diffuse use of the term in the Federal Republic until the 1970s, which I pointed to earlier. Modernity was such a popular and proven term, that it did not need to be precisely defined. And the only prominent concept of modernity developed so far – by Adorno in his *Aesthetic Theory* published in 1970 – still upheld the traditional primacy of aesthetic modernity and was quite ambiguous with respect to the other dimensions of modernity, Adorno being very sceptical about modernity's social and political perspectives. Now however, since the newcomer 'postmodernity' had put 'modernity' on the defensive, the latter had to be effectively conceptualized or vanish. Habermas took up the task. Only from then on was the use of the term 'modernity' more than just a popular slogan: it now signalled support for a well-defined programme. Of course it needs to be added that both postmodernity and modernity are interpretative concepts, which means that they do not simply describe, but advocate an object, and by doing so transform or even help to create this object. Such terms, like all proper terms for self-description, are descriptive and transformative at the same time.

3. *Postmodernity versus Modernity?*

What is the core of postmodernity, and what became the core of modernity during these discussions around 1980?

a. Postmodernity (Lyotard) 'Simplifying to the extreme', Lyotard said, one could define 'postmodern' 'as incredulity toward metanarratives'.[35] The dominance of such metanarratives had been characteristic for modernity. Metanarratives like emancipation through science during the Enlightenment, teleology of the spirit in Idealism, liberation of mankind by proletarian revolution in Marxism, ubiquitous happiness through wealth in capitalism, each claimed to cover every sphere of knowledge and life, and to solve – at least in the long run – all problems. But the successive failure of these metanarratives, so postmodernism argues, is due to a systematic flaw in their claim for totality. The totalizing approach neglects on principle the diversity of types of rationality, as at least theoretical, ethical and aesthetic rationality are to be distinguished, these types being irreducible to one single type; and equally it ignores the diversity of cultures, language games and life-forms, which certainly are not different in all aspects, but are incommensurable in some basic respects, so that their diversity cannot altogether be overcome – except by means of ignorance or terror. The flaw of metanarratives is the same in each case. The claim for totality can be raised only by rendering one type of rationality, or culture, or life absolute. This basic error engenders open or hidden terrorism, but also finally the breakdown of these metanarratives. Insight into the insurmountability and legitimacy of diversity, and the emotional acceptance and affirmation of plurality constitutes the postmodern consciousness and mood.

Postmodernism accepts and advocates diversity in knowledge and art, in culture and society in general – including the resulting conflicts, contradictions, and basic disagreements. It aims, as Lyotard put it, at 'a politics that would respect both the desire for justice and the desire for the unknown',[36] and at 'a humanity [. . .] which is sensitive to the heterogeneous ends implied in the various known and unknown genres of discourse, and capable of pursuing them as much as possible'.[37]

b. Modernity (Habermas) Habermas characterized this postmodern effort as a move towards irrationalism and neo-conservatism.

Modernists like Habermas apparently cannot perceive the pluralization of rationality – at least beyond a certain extent – in terms other than those of irrationality, and they do not seem to be able to see in criticism of modernity anything other than conservatism. Lyotard, on the contrary, claimed to be more rational and less conservative than Habermas himself, the Habermasian neglect of the modern pluralization of rationality itself blurring rationality, and Habermas's mere defence of good old modernity clearly being conservative rather than modern.

According to Habermas, modernity has indeed created considerable problems. Yet they are not to be cured by a resort to postmodernism, but by a return to the project of the Enlightenment and its modern renewal. The problems of modernity all have a common denominator: division. There is a – basically acceptable – uncoupling of system and life-world, followed by the separation of economy and bureaucracy within the system and an opposition between traditionally imposed versus communicatively achieved orientation within the life-world. But then, within the life-world, a further series of dangerous divisions occurs: first the splitting off of science, morality and art from everyday life, secondly the growing separation of these expert cultures one from another, and thirdly the impoverishment and fragmentation of everyday consciousness, which is deprived of any exchange with the expert cultures. The far-reaching fragmentation of the life-world finally results in the 'colonization of the life-world' by the system – with the life-world now being, so to speak, the new, Habermasian proletariat victimized by the system.[38]

As all these problems are caused by exaggerated divisions, the proper and universal remedy lies in new and intense forms of mediation. Hence Habermas advocates the regaining of unity between the differentiated types of rationality and a recoupling of everyday practice and expert cultures. Thus the life-world could again become strong enough to resist its colonization by the system, and finally a 'reconciliation of modernity' would be the happy result.

Generally speaking, Habermas does not want differentiation to be eliminated, but he wants to complete it through processes of mediation, unification and reconciliation. No longer a metaphysical, but a modern, thinker Habermas does not presuppose a unity in reason or society; but as a modern, not a postmodern, thinker he still sticks to Hegel's claim that true reason and society finally demand unity, and he believes – as opposed to postmodernism – that this unity can be achieved despite, and beyond the apparent diversity of, and within, cultures by means of communication – this being Habermas's metanarrative.

So far, the contrast between modernity and postmodernity is, very generally speaking, the choice between ultimate unity or diversity, and, in practical terms, the decision either for a renewal of the project of modernity or for a shift to postmodernity.

c. The Intertwining of Modernity and Postmodernity   But now let me question this pattern.[39] The strict dichotomy of modernity and postmodernity is, viewed in the international context of the debate, a particularly German feature. It constitutes the fundamental mistake in this debate, for it implies a basic misunderstanding of postmodernity. Postmodernity is not opposed to modernity altogether. This is, first of all, due to the fact that within modernity there exist different versions of modernity – differing in time-span and content. The term 'modernity' can refer to the project of modern science of *mathesis universalis* as established in the seventeenth century by Galileo and Descartes; or to the social and political Enlightenment modernity since the eighteenth century; or to the progress of industrialization since the nineteenth century; or to aesthetic modernity as it was simultaneously – but contrastingly – defined by Baudelaire; or to the different goals of the twentieth century's artistic and scientific avant-gardes on the one hand, and political totalitarianisms on the other hand.

Postmodernity shares certain options of modernity and is opposed to others within this all-too-manifold frame of modernity. Postmodernism criticizes all totalizing versions – all 'one-fits-all'-versions – of modernity – for example the scientific one set up in the seventeenth century or the underlying cognitivism of the Enlightenment – as well as obvious political totalitarianism of whatever kind, but also the smooth forms of social homogenization due to the culture industry or the current predominance of digitalized information. On the other hand, postmodernism clearly advocates alternative currents and contents in modernity like the democratic impulses of the Enlightenment, or the turn to plurality in the arts and the revolutions in science in this century.[40] Lyotard has always pointed out that postmodernism understands itself as the heir to the artistic and scientific avant-garde from the beginning of this century, and that it was quite possible to be postmodern within or even before modernity – Diderot or Montaigne being prominent examples.

What can we conclude from this? Firstly: there is no strict distinction, rather there is intertwining between modernity and postmodernity. Second: whenever we hear 'postmodernity', we should ask: 'Post which type of modernity does postmodernity claim to be?' A great deal of fuss has been made about the supposed unclearness of the meaning of 'postmodernity'. But postmodernism has been wrongly blamed for this. The unclearness is basically due to the reference term 'modernity' – this already covering a variety of different and even contradictory kinds of modernity. And a third conclusion would be: none of the contents of postmodernity first begins with postmodernity. Each of them was already implied in at least one type of modernity. Hence postmodernity signifies rather a shift in emphasis – the accent now moving from unity and totality to plurality and diversity – than a break between epochs. The suggestion of a strict separation between modernity and postmodernity, the latter constituting a new epoch, is rather the core fallacy in the whole debate. The claim to a new epoch was never made by any of the postmodern thinkers; it is an invention of modernists to serve their purposes. Finally, postmodernity can best be understood as the current transformation of modernity, making the formerly more implicit acknowledgement of diversity now undoubtedly explicit. This is what I suggested in my book in 1987, whose title *Unsere postmoderne Moderne* ('Our Postmodern Modern') tries to indicate the intertwining of modernity and postmodernity and to argue that the term 'postmodern' stands precisely for the traits we need to develop in order to attain the modernity of present times. We should get rid of the supposed dualism of modernity and postmodernity, and concentrate not on the notions, but on the contents.

4. *Details of the Debate in the Federal Republic*

In presenting the German debate, I have thus far attempted to clarify the concept of postmodernity and its relation to modernity. Now I shall turn to some specific details of the German debate.

a. An Outrageous Attack For some German critics, postmodernism was connected not only with irrationalism and neoconservatism, but – even worse – with fascism. This is, for understandable reasons, the most devastating reproach one can raise in contemporary Germany's intellectual debates. Remember that since the debates about modern art in the early Federal Republic, modernity was understood to be a bulwark against the return of fascism, and that therefore any critique of modernism was suspected of being an attack on that bulwark. This constellation – a sort of archetype in the psychic structure of the Federal Republic – reappeared during the late 1970s in the discussion about the New State Gallery in Stuttgart, with Behnisch being praised as representing the good German tradition of modern architecture, totally repressing the fact that this tradition had very successfully, and even in the best functionalist spirit, been appropriated by National Socialism, whereas Stirling was accused of being a new 'fascist' architect.

In 1988, the pattern was applied to the controversy between modern and postmodern philosophy by Manfred Frank, formerly a professor of literature and now of philosophy. In two articles in the *Frankfurter Rundschau* and the *Frankfurter Allgemeine Zeitung*, Frank accused the German advocates of French postmodern philosophy of reintroducing prefascist, cryptofascist or straightforward fascist thinking.[41] Frank considered his attack as a necessary case of unmasking. As the postmodern anti-modernism now came from France it was, according to Frank, largely protected against being recognized as a renewal of Germany's own dangerous tradition. It was easier to readopt this very tradition through the French filter. Postmodernism, Frank wanted to make us believe, is a return of prefascism or neofascism.[42]

I can hardly express how grotesque this appears to me. I would like to analyse Frank's articles period by period, presenting them as examples of concept politics. Instead of doing this, let me – for reasons of time – just mention two points. First: Lyotard's principal work, *Le Différend* from 1983, was from the first to the last page a book about and against Auschwitz, the contrast between the suppressed Jewish and the dominant Graeco-German tradition of thinking always being one of Lyotard's guiding-lines. Secondly: I want to reply to Frank's attack by considering the relationship between postmodernity and democracy.

It is obvious, in my view, that the postmodern recognition and defence of diversity is based on the affirmation, and represents a reinforcement of the principles, of democracy. Postmodernism claims that democracy is a form of social organization that is aware of basic conflicts and that is needed precisely for a situation of basic dissent instead of basic agreement within a society. Human and civil rights – which have their sense exactly in allowing and respecting such dissent – are the only common basis. And they obviously represent the normative core of postmodernism's move towards diversity and conflict. Therefore postmodernism's orientation to dissent – instead of the modern and particularly Habermasian orientation to consent – seems to be evidence of postmodernism's trying to realize the basic feature of democracy more radically than conventional modernism did.[43]

Of course, there are exaggerations and silly versions within the field of postmodernism, but there are equally misleading versions within the modernist strand too. It would be inappropriate to compare bad postmodern to good modern versions or vice versa. We have to compare the respective principles, not their deviations.

Postmodernism has not been fortunate in the Federal Republic. Its misleading image shaped by Habermas and his followers like Frank prevailed. You should not be connected with postmodernism if you want to be a respectable person in Germany. (I suspect Germany and Britain have some things in common.)

b. The Hidden Success of Postmodernism   On the non-terminological level, however – on the factual level – postmodernism won the race. Modernists today draw a very postmodern image of their beloved modernity. Let me give an example.

When in 1966 Robert Venturi published his manifesto *Complexity and Contradiction in Architecture*, his views were regarded as a scandalous betrayal of modernity. But in 1989, a review of recent books on modern architecture pointed out that the common denominator in new diagnoses was the attribution of complexity and contradiction to modern architecture. Whereas in 1966 modernist experts had said: Venturi is advocating horrible ideas, let us reject them and continue the path of modernity which is so wonderfully opposed to that nonsense, they now, some twenty years later – with postmodern architecture having meanwhile become a success – have rewritten history and presented a totally different image of modern architecture. They have declared that modern architecture had already been deeply characterized by complexity and contradiction. (Which, by the way, also serves another purpose: you do not need postmodernism, but can just continue modernism.)

Well, paper won't blush. It patiently accepts too the analogous rewriting of philosophical modernity, as it is being undertaken today: modernists miraculously discovering all the reasonable demands of postmodernity as permanent demands already made by modernity. In this sense, I am saying that postmodernism may have lost most of the battles, but has won the war. The concept and the term 'postmodernity' are still disliked amidst the dominant intellectual circles in the Federal Republic, but most of postmodernism's suggestions have been adopted. And beyond the intellectual sphere postmodernism is largely accepted anyway.

Finally, it is not the terms, but the contents that count. We might very well do without the term 'postmodernity' – and will probably do so once its contents have been realized. As a provocation, the term was useful. Currently, the remission of the struggle about postmodernity may indicate an increasing acknowledgement of its contents.

5. *Views on Postmodernity in the Democratic Republic*

What about postmodernism in the German Democratic Republic? It is not surprising that postmodernism was rejected by the official culture and politics. It was recognized as being a concept criticizing the totalizing claims of Marxism and the oppressive structure of the political system. For the same reason, it was welcomed and adopted by some opposition intellectuals. The most famous example is Heiner Müller, who, in his dramatic pieces from the mid-1960s onwards, had developed an impressive critique of the system, and who in 1979 during a conference in New York on *The Question of Postmodernism* attacked some principles of modernity.[44] The younger generation of authors born since the 1950s – authors like Uwe Kolbe, Michael Wüstenfeld and Fritz-Hendrik Melle – have taken leave of the utopian claims of modernity and therefore deny both the conformist and the oppositional utopian stances of Christa Wolf and Hermann Kant on the one side, and Volker Braun and Wolf Biermann on the other. In their own writing they combine premodern, modern and new styles in an obviously postmodern manner. In the musical sphere during the late 1980s it even became popular to describe compositions as 'postmodern'.

In Eastern Europe in general, postmodernism was largely welcomed by opponents of the system. Postmodernism, with its attack on totality and its defence of diversity, provided just the type of critique which met the requirements of opposition within these systems. Postmodernism is appreciated for its critical force against political and cultural monopolism, against all sorts of 'one-fits-all' doctrines. It is surprising how many translations of Western postmodern articles and books were published in Eastern Europe even before 1991; as an author you often get to know about them only by chance. The critical potential of postmodernism was much better understood in the East than in the West.

6.   *Were the two German States in fact Postmodern?*

But so far, I have only been considering the operative use of the term 'postmodernity' – what about its reflective applicability? Were the Federal Republic and the Democratic Republic – beyond the usage of the label 'postmodern' – in fact postmodern societies, at least to a certain extent?

Under the cover of a socialist society, a variety of specific life-forms developed in the German Democratic Republic. People had to take care of several everyday needs and problems by themselves, and they did so by building networks connecting people who shared specific interests, orientations and difficulties. To this extent, the GDR-society was postmodern on a micro-social level. But there was, of course, no political or legal acknowledgement of this diversity. The GDR was possibly postmodern on the factual level, but not on one of rights. And the mentality in general – which is in my view an equally important point – was not well-disposed to plurality or diversity, either on the level of the state or on the level of the networks and groups.[45]

In the Federal Republic, there was both a legal acknowledgement of, and existing cultural and social diversity. But what about the third dimension I just introduced, the mental preparedness for plurality and the appreciation of differences? This, I'm afraid, is the sore point in both former parts of Germany.

The legal and democratic acknowledgement of differences in the Federal Republic proved to be somehow unavailing as soon as social plurality increased, which was the case after Western Germany had welcomed millions of so-called 'guest-workers', and had later become an immigration country. Aggression, not acknowledgement, was the order of the day.

Unification itself was an example of the modernist attitude, not the postmodern capacity of the old Federal Republic. The combination of two different social patterns within one society would have been an exemplary postmodern opportunity, but in fact Unification really did credit to its, significantly, modern name: all that occurred was the absorption of one system by the other – not at all the beginning of a postmodern patchwork. Even obviously creditable patterns of the GDR-tradition were not adopted without alteration – which considerably hurt the Eastern newcomers.

After 1990, cases of hidden and open aggression towards foreigners as well as other Germans multiplied. I am afraid there is simply too little liberal tradition in Germany, too little liberality embodied in German mentality. When German intellectuals today claim that the German democracy is one of the strongest in the world, and that the legal system guarantees the prosecution of all infractions, including aggression towards foreigners, and, surprisingly enough, even people from the 1968 student revolt are currently arguing this way, they miss – I think – the real point: the necessity of liberal standards in everyday practice. What foreigners need is everyday acknowledgement – when they interact with local authorities, look for an appartment, or simply go shopping – not the chance to win a case three years later. German brains and hearts have hardly ever become open to plurality.[16]

7.   *Ethnicity or Transculturality?*

Finally, I would like to raise another point with respect to future developments.

What I feel in Eastern Germany today is – once more – a desire for clear-cut orientation, for another kind of 'one-fits-all' orientation. Transformation and heterogeneity seem difficult to bear. Despite all former experiences, homogeneity is again becoming the dream. In Western Germany similar tendencies arise. But the return of fundamentalism – which is the clearest opponent of postmodernism – obviously is not a specifically German, but a worldwide problem today.

Under pressure, people tend to take a step backwards, not forwards. Ethnic self-definitions, homogenizing versions of nationalism become appealing again. Formerly, as long as a politics of unification, imposed from outside, prevailed – as was the case in Eastern Europe until 1991 – such regressive options may have had a progressive impact. They were able to provide points of resistance. Yet the danger was that, once they had won and become the guiding-line of the new state without any alternation – especially without opening themselves to plurality – they just replaced the former external repression, by a new, inner repression.

But today ethnicity and tribal claims reappear under different conditions: not because of external repression, but because of inner economic challenges – increasing unemployment, transfer of production to other countries, etc. – and in view of the difficult demands of transformation. In these conditions, I believe, the return to ethnicity and tribalism is just the wrong move. The task would rather be to recognize the current cultural intertwining – no unitary single culture exists unalloyed any more. One of the main missions of cultural analysis today, it seems to me, consists in the elaboration of the transcultural design of today's cultures.[47] This too is one of postmodernism's perspectives, and, perhaps, the most promising one and the one we should pursue in the future.

Notes

1. In trying to cover both topics indicated in the title – modernity as well as postmodernity – and to consider the whole period of post-war Germany, I will, of course, have to be selective.
2. Molière, *Le Bourgeois gentilhomme*, Act II, Scene i.
3. 'Wir schaffen das moderne Deutschland.'
4. 'Auf den Kanzler kommt es an.'
5. Haftmann had just published his very influential book on *Painting in the Twentieth Century*, New York, 1960, 2 vols; first German edition: *Malerei im 20. Jahrhundert*, Munich, 1954, 2 Bde.
6. Even if we don't accept this avant-garde reconstruction of art history any more, we must admit that it provided a very convincing and powerful meta-narrative in the history of art in the twentieth century.
7. This, by the way, fits German tradition very well: the German term 'die Moderne' being first used with respect to literature, which didn't occur until 1887: Eugen Wolff, 'Thesen zur literarischen Moderne', in *Allgemeine Deutsche Universitätszeitung*, Jg. 1, Nr. 1, 1. Jan. 1887, p. 10.
8. 'Der Magen knurrt, doch die Augen blitzen.'; Christoph Kleßmann, 'Das Haus wurde gebaut aus den Steinen, die vorhanden waren – Zur kulturgeschichtlichen Kontinuitätsdiskussion nach 1945', *Tel Aviver Jahrbuch für deutsche Geschichte*, Vol. XIX, 1990, pp. 159–77, p. 167.
9. It also renewed the tradition of Catholic anti-modernism from the beginning of the century.
10. It seems noteworthy to me, that this perception of modernism – however ideological its evaluation may be – covers one basic point: the correspondence between modern art and principles of the West, modern art being perceived as a focus of Western modernity.

11. Ralf Dahrendorf, *Society and Democracy in Germany*, New York, 1967, p. 424.

12. Ibid., p. 111.

13. Looking at the operative use of the term 'modernity', it was correct to say that, in 1965, there was 'no political party that had made modernity the keynote of its programme and none that consistently worked for it without saying so' (ibid., p. 437); but in a reflective perspective the Federal Republic was a notably modern society and has been increasingly so ever since. And already in 1965 Dahrendorf recognized that despite the 'traces of restoration [...] authoritarianism of the traditional kind has become impossible in German society' (ibid., p. 438).

14. Even in the 1950s, in German journalism and in relation to the prevalence of economic and technical progress, the Federal Republic was reflectively characterized as a 'modern industrial society', Hans-Peter Schwarz, *Die Ära Adenauer. Gründerjahre der Republik, 1949–1957*, Stuttgart – Wiesbaden, 1981, p. 389.

15. Klaus Hildebrand, *Von Erhard zur Großen Koalition, 1963–1969*, Stuttgart – Wiesbaden, 1984, p. 438.

16. Dahrendorf, *Society and Democracy in Germany*, p. 424.

17. Ibid., p. 422, 424. Yet this was the case only in principle, with considerable deviations in reality, remember for example the new privileges of the party caste.

18. Ibid., p. 422.

19. Ibid., p. 423.

20. Interestingly, it was also from the late 1970s onwards that a reform of socialism came to be contemplated which made explicit use of the word 'modernization' and helped itself to the political contents of Western modernity. This, of course, tended to occur under cover. Intellectuals such as Hans-Peter Krüger and Wolfgang Engler attempted to use analysis of Western modernity in a new fomulation of the prospects for socialist reform. From 1988 onwards, the 'modern socialism' project (Michael Brie, Dieter Segert, Rainer Land *inter alios*) examined a reform of real socialism with recourse to basic ideas of Western modernity such as parliamentary democracy, separation of powers and the emancipatory potential of capitalism. Socialism – which until then had been understood to be a contra-modernity project – was now – by taking on board 'modern' elements understood, or turned around to be, emancipatory – to be reformed. Of course, the thought in this was not of an assimilation; the question was still to be one of socialism, and a move towards the side of civil rights activists remained excluded. This 'conspiratorial avant-gardism' was however infused with a great deal of ambivalence – just as much in theory as in practice. See on these movements: Rainer Land and Ralf Possenkehl,

'Namenlose Stimmen waren uns voraus. Politische Diskurse von Intellekutellen aus der DDR', *Herausforderung. Historisch-politische Analysen*, ed. Wolfgang Schmale, vol. 1, Bochum, 1994, especially 'Der "konspirative Avantagardismus" der dritten SED Generation', pp. 36–48. The most ambitious attempt to reconcile socialism and the constitutional state was undertaken by Rosi Will, 'Rechtsstaatlichkeit als Moment demokratischer politischer Machtausübung', *Deutsche Zeitschrift für Philosophie*, 37 (1989), pp. 801–12.

21. Dahrendorf, *Society and Democracy in Germany*, p. 422.

22. Ibid., p. 405, esp. p. 403.

23. Amitai Etzioni, *The Active Society. A Theory of Societal and Political Processes*, London – New York, 1968, pp. vii, 561, 573, 576, esp. Chapter 16: The Morphology of Modern and Post-Modern Societies, pp. 432–65.

24. Ibid., Preface, p. viii.

25. Jean-François Lyotard, *The Postmodern Condition: A Report on Knowledge*, Minneapolis, 1984, p. 40.

26. Ibid., p. 41.

27. Once again, art was the avant-garde sphere – although it was precisely avant-gardism which was now brought into question.

28. Irving Howe, 'Mass Society and Postmodern Fiction', *Partisan Review* XXVI (1959), pp. 420–36. Harry Levin, 'What Was Modernism?', *Massachusetts Review*, I, 4 (1960), pp. 609–30.

29. Leslie Fiedler, 'Cross the Border – Close the Gap', *The Collected Essays of Leslie Fiedler*, Vol. II, New York, 1971, pp. 461–85.

30. Ibid., p. 479.

31. Ibid., p. 485.

32. Charles Jencks, *The Language of Post-Modern Architecture*, New York – London, 1977, p. 6. According to Jencks, 'a post-modern building [. . .] speaks on at least two levels at once: to other architects and a concerned minority who care about specifically architectural meanings, and to the public at large' (ibid.).

33. Robert Venturi, *Complexity and Contradiction in Architecture*, New York, 1966.

34. In English, the speech was published under the title 'Modernity versus Postmodernity', *New German Critique*, 22, 1981, pp. 3–14.

35. Lyotard, *The Postmodern Condition*, Introduction, p. xxiv.

36. Ibid., p. 67.

37. Jean-François Lyotard, *The Different: Phrases in Dispute*, Minneapolis, 1988, p. 178 [§ 253]. 'Justice would consist in recognizing, not reducing the plurality, specificity, autonomy and untranslatability of interlocking language-games.' Dialogue with Jean-Pierre Dubost, published as an appendix to the first German edition: *Das postmoderne Wissen: Ein Bericht*, Bremen, 1982, pp. 127-50, p. 131.

38. Jürgen Habermas, *The Theory of Communicative Action*, 2 vols, Boston, 1989.

39. I first developed this view in my book *Unsere postmoderne Moderne*, Weinheim, 1987; 4th edn, Berlin 1994; English edn, *Our Postmodern Modern*, New Brunswick, NJ, 1995.

40. I have focused on the relation to art in my article, 'The Birth of Postmodern Philosophy from the Spirit of Modern Art', *History of European Ideas*, Vol. 14, No. 3, 1992, pp. 379–98.

41. Manfred Frank, 'Kleiner (Tübinger) Programmentwurf', *Frankfurter Rundschau*, 5. März 1988, p. ZB 3; idem, 'Zweifacher Auftritt. Die Bewegung der deutschen Philosophie', *Frankfurter Allgemeine Zeitung*, 29 June 1988, No. 148, p. 33 *passim*.

42. Frank is reproducing the type of critique inaugurated by Allan Bloom, *The Closing of the American Mind*, New York, 1987 in the USA and Luc Ferry and Alain Renaut in France: *French Philosophy of the Sixties: An Essay on Antihumanism*, Amherst, 1990: in both cases the influence of bad German tradition was blamed for the destruction of the respective country's cultural and intellectual standards. I have given a more detailed criticism of Frank's view in my article, 'Rückblickend auf einen Streit, der ein Widerstreit bleibt – Ein letztes Mal: Moderne versus Postmoderne', in Armin Wildermuth and Ulrike Klein (eds), *Postmoderne – Ende in Sicht*, Heiden, 1990, pp. 1–25.

43. This is, incidentally, another example of the intertwining of postmodernism and modernity, postmodernism adopting and radicalizing the modern principle of democracy.

44. Heiner Müller, 'Der Schrecken ist die erste Erscheinung des Neuen. Zu einer Diskussion über Postmodernismus in New York', in Heiner Müller, *Rotwelsch*, Berlin, 1982, pp. 94–8.

45. Guest-workers in the GDR were located in ghettos; visitors from fellow socialist countries often complained about the animosity of GDR citizens; and the networks were highly homogenizing.

46. This would perhaps be the proper way to reformulate Dahrendorf's former complaint about the German 'attitude of traditionalism' in contemporary terms.

47. I have developed the concept of transculturality in various articles, e.g.: 'Transkulturalität – die veränderte Verfassung heutiger Kulturen', *Sichtweisen. Die Vielheit in der Einheit*, Weimar, 1994, pp. 83–122. Additional aspects are contained in my book *Vernunft: Die zeitgenössische Vernunftkritik und das Konzept der transversalen Vernunft*, Frankfurt a.M., 1995.

JENS REICH

East Germany: Mentality Five Years after Unification

With the title of this chapter I may have fallen into a well-known trap: I am not sure whether the word 'mentality' has a connotation sufficiently similar in English to its German cognate's usage to make them synonymous. When proposing the title I had of course the German *Mentalität* in mind. Now, on reflection, I have doubts.

My understanding of 'mentality' is close to the German words *Sinnesart*, *Denkweise* and *Denkungsart*, i.e. a mode of outlook on everyday societal and political issues. It is only distantly related to intellectual disposition and likewise distantly to emotion; it has some connection to the public 'mood' as well as to political emotions. It is something that prevails in a population rather than in its individuals, it need not be dominant in that group, but somehow dominates the public sentiment. Only 20 per cent of the East German population votes for the post-communist party (PDS), but the motivation for this minority behaviour is something that dominates public sentiment. Such mentality is something different from the political or economic situation, but related to it through causal links and correlation. It is best described by examples, and I will try to do just this and to leave generalizations to the work of people specializing in sociology.

Anybody travelling in a relaxed mood and with open mind through Germany cannot escape noticing a discontinuity when crossing the previous border between the two German states. Now, five years after unification, there many places where the former demarcation line is difficult to detect. Especially in Berlin the Wall has been dismantled with such German thoroughness that not even remnants have been preserved for purposes of touristic entertainment, much to the regret of travel offices and hotels. The only section left, at *Bernauer Straße*, is being claimed as property to be returned to a parish whose erstwhile graveyard was levelled off by the communist authorities after the construction of the wall in 1961. The claim appears to be well founded and likely to succeed, so we will probably not be able to show to our grandchildren that impressive structure which shaped our lives to such an extent that whole generations were literally 'wall-sick', i.e. in a state of melancholic depression about their boring existence, surrounded by an impenetrable border that only the privileged could pass, and even they only at a considerable price of moral or mental contortion.

Notwithstanding this disappearance of a concrete memorial, it is the contrast in lifestyle and mentality in the two Germanies that strikes the attention of the observer. There are still enormous differences in the social and economic constitution of both parts, East and West, that contribute to the maintenance of the mentality gap, but these are fading away. East Germany is now definitely recovering and will slowly catch up. To analyse this aspect would mean going through accumulations of statistical data. I will abstain from this, as I believe that the mental rift, the 'wall in the heads' as it has been aptly if somewhat exaggeratedly described, is more interesting and more persistent than those more superficial symptoms. In short, I do not believe that economic activity is the only determining factor of mentality.

I have not undertaken systematic studies on mentality in the two parts of unified Germany. I have rather noted my experience in passing.

I live in East Berlin, incidentally: please, release me from the obligation always to add the politically correct 'former' when referring to anything connected to the deceased German Democratic Republic – East Berlin and the GDR and all that is a historic reality as is the Roman Empire, and there is no need to stress its disappearance in every proposition: I have lived for the greater part of my life in that state, and the incantation of its current formerness appears to me to be a psychic mechanism to repress its continued existence in our minds. I live in Berlin, I said, as an alien fish in PDS waters. PDS, the Party of Democratic Socialism, is the rallying point for many people who were either opposed to or disappointed by German unification and the dismantling of Socialism, and I am living in a stronghold of that political movement.

Our constituency was one of the four that directly returned PDS candidates to the Bonn parliament, i.e. by a majority of constituency votes, a fact which according to German electoral law suspends the five per cent hurdle for that party and carries all other votes nationwide proportionally into the Bundestag. This means that about 40 to 50 per cent of all persons I meet in our institute's canteen or in the supermarket round the corner are voters for that party, which is a direct successor organization to the old Socialist Unity Party – the SED – under Ulbricht's and Honecker's leadership. Most of the voters and many of the members do not wish to return to the state of affairs before 1989, but they remain in a state of obstinate opposition to the new state and its societal formation. Their permanent complaints about almost everything that went wrong or is going wrong, rounded off with an emphatic 'Now you see, this system cannot manage it either!', are certainly not an expression of majority opinion, but they dominate the public sphere. Other political parties are clearly on the defensive against this. The reply 'You keep quiet, you had 40 years to sort things out!' was very effective in 1990, but has lost much of its force in the five years since 1990 under Helmut Kohl's leadership.

In January 1990, in a discussion with Polish *Solidarnosc* activists of the 1970s and 1980s, Adam Michnik warned us of the imminent change of mood. 'They will reproach you that matters used to be better under communism!' he said. I did not believe for a moment that this would apply to East Germany, and expected that the old brigade would soon exit from the political scene. But this proved to be wrong. The PDS doubled its vote from approximately one million in 1990 to two million in 1994. It is a particularly surprising phenomenon that even people who would never vote for that party, including myself, nevertheless maintain that it would not be good if these two million protest votes were not represented politically. Voters would go off in a huff and point out to everybody that 'this is no democracy at all'. All my channels of information are reporting that in the new *Bundesländer* most of the people calmly accept that Gregor Gysi and his crew are now again in the *Bundestag*, to the considerable annoyance of Helmut Kohl, who, in 1990 certainly expected them to dwindle away in the wave of reconstruction and recovery that he predicted for the immediate future.

I am now more cautious about any prediction that the PDS will be a transitory phenomenon. It has obviously something to do with the East German mentality, and is therefore rooted more deeply than a superficial analysis would tend to maintain. The PDS is not just the rallying-point of the losers of 1990. It is more.

A closer analysis of the election returns of the PDS reveals differences more subtle than just a clear-cut East–West rift. To be sure, that party has gained around twenty per cent of the votes in all the new *Länder*, while it was well below three per cent in all the old *Länder*. But on closer scrutiny an uneven distribution appears. The Elbe river cuts through the old GDR territory like a diagonal, from north-west to south-east, from Hamburg to Dresden. The turnout of the PDS varies along a line perpendicular to the Elbe, i.e. from north-east to south-west. The lowest percentages were obtained in the south, i.e. Thuringia and parts of Saxony. The highest outcomes were in the north-east. East Berlin is something of an exception, because it harbours many of the functionaries and élites of the old regime. Thus, by and large, the protest votes for the PDS and the accompanying anti-Western mood are more or less an East-Elbian phenomenon, and as such have roots reaching back far farther into German history than the 45 years under communist rule.

The Elbe was in previous centuries the dividing line between *Grundherrschaft* and *Gutsherrschaft*. I have difficulties in describing the difference in English, but the main difference is that in the West the peasants with no property of their own had their farmland on lease from the lord of the manor, while in the East they were forced into personal serfdom, bound to the land which they cultivated. After liberation, i.e. after Napoleon, this century-old situation was transformed so that in the West there were independent farmers, by contrast with farmworkers on the lord of the manor's land in the East. This difference has left deep traces in the whole culture and lifestyle, as well as in the mentality, of the rural populations east and west of the Elbe river. And it has transformed the mentality of the urban population, which was formed in the nineteenth century when the rural exodus drove it into the cities.

As recently as in GDR times one could notice this fundamental difference immediately when comparing, for instance, a Thuringian village with a Pomeranian one in the north. The typical Thuringian or Saxon village has a historic structure, with church, village green, streets and side-alleys, the farm estates with stables inside the village, but facing the street with a garden and a decorated door. Extrovert, inviting a visit. The arable land tends to be outside the village. The typical East-Elbian village, on the other hand, consists of one very long street, the farm houses closed, introvert, being preferably entered from the yard side, with a strip of land beyond the barn. The land outside the village was as a rule owned by the landowner. Many villages are just farmworkers' settlements annexed to the landlord's estate and dominated by the manor, a constellation you rarely find westward of the Elbe river. In GDR times either farmlands were forced together in the so-called LPG's (agricultural co-operatives), or an old estate was transformed into a state farm run by wage-workers. Both these types of unit have been largely dissolved since unification. Only a small number of farmers returned to any form of private farming. Others tried to establish reformed co-operative enterprises. Many of the state-owned former estates have meanwhile been privatized, with the bidding dominated by the pre-GDR landowners who were preferred by the *Treuhand Gesellschaft*.

I have often heard the slogan *Bauernland in Junkerhand* (farmers' land in the squire's hand) as an inversion of the saying *Junkerland in Bauernhand* prevailing in the late 1940s, when the landowners were dispossessed by the land reform carried out by the Soviet authorities. In one Mecklenburg village the new landowner came by with a tractor and dragged a voluminous sandstone memorial to the GDR land reform into the nearby lake. This infuriated the local population, and they rented another tractor to drag it back to its place in the centre of the village. This is class struggle of a novel kind!

I describe all this history because it is reflected in the behavioural stereotypes of the population, to the south and north of that Elbe line. In Saxony or in the mountains, when you enter a village inn you will be addressed by the guests and the owner. In the north distance is usually preserved. They tend to mistrust you as an urbanite. You can live for decades in a village of Mecklenburg and are still a stranger. West of the Elbe people tend to welcome the restitution of land or of a castle to the former owner. They welcome him as an investor bringing work and capital into the place. In East-Elbia they tend to reject the *Junker* (squire) and appear to prefer to leave the village untouched in its state of decay after the downfall of socialist agriculture. I describe tendencies, of course – there are always exceptions. By and large, however, I think I am right in emphasizing that there are historical roots to the East–West resentment, and that the Elbe river is the borderline rather than the old demarcation line, which extends further to the West and South. And what I have described for the countryside, applies *mutatis mutandis* also to the towns and cities. The industrialization in Saxony, for instance, has a longer tradition and was based on middle-class enterprise. In the north, industry was closely related to agriculture and often in landowners' hands: the typical case was a beet sugar refinery, or a capitalist enterprise not owned by the local middle class.

Along with all this comes the notion that the population of Saxony and Thuringia is traditionally more flexible, agile, adaptable, enterprising and clever than people in the north. You hear this already in the dialect: ponderous and slow in the north, and quick and versatile in the south. You will rarely hear the heavy-going northern accent in the south or in Berlin, which, as a metropolitan city, is similar to Saxony with respect to social buoyancy, while Saxon intonation is quite common in the north. Herr Günter Krause, for instance, having been an MP from the furthest north in the 1990 *Volkskammer* and later on in the *Bundestag*, made a rapid career in Bonn and became minister of transport in Kohl's cabinet, until he stumbled over a matter of business and had to resign. He then became a banker for some time afterwards, failed again, but is still an entrepreneur – one of the very few Easterners successful after unification. Needless to say his accent is strongly Anhaltian, from the west of the GDR, he went northward from his origins in Halle. It is a common saying that during the GDR Saxony exported all its Party and Stasi bigwigs to Berlin, where the Saxon accent is quite common, although extremely unpopular, so that Berlin now harbours all the Saxon PDS voters; while Saxony profits by that purification, and now votes overwhelmingly for Herr Biedenkopf, a Christian Democrat – behaviour which is certainly an advantage before the throne of Herr Kohl in Bonn.

Apart from traditional character traits of the population which contribute to the Eastern mentality after unification, there is a substantial legacy from GDR socialization – which lasted, after all, for at least two full generations. This is a sediment more recent than those historic traits, but also fully present, and it is very difficult to forecast how long it will survive the social and economic union of the two Germanies. Again, it comprises lifestyle and behavioural stereotypes, but this time also the intellectual outlook on political events.

East Germany in its early period was a satellite of the Soviet Union with a dictatorial Stalinist regime that profited much from the submissive reflexes of the population, which had been developed as early as the Imperial decades, after Bismarck's unification, and were confirmed during the Hitler period. The main effect of the years from 1945 until the construction of the wall in 1961 was the destruction, dissolution or expulsion of the old bourgeoisie: enterprise-owning, estate-owning, educated élites, and nearly all middle-class strata. My family belonged to that class, and I lived through that process during my youth. It is still in my memory. What remained was the petty bourgeoisie, as flexible and indestructible as always. Their lifestyle and mentality diffused into the new, originally proletarian, power élite, and the replacement of the old functional élites opened career avenues for the former lower middle class. The GDR was, in the words of the writer Günter Gaus, the state of the *Kleine Leute* (little people). Of the 'philistine people', I would add. I could tell long stories about the philosophy of everyday life in East Germany, but that is not our topic today.

The result of the second, middle, post-Stalinist phase of that country's development was the coming to full growth of a ruling class so far as political and economic power were concerned, but without that power being reflected in cultural dominance. In a very dialectical way the petty-bourgeois archetype, which aroused such wrath in Karl Marx, gained the upper hand, imbued the whole society with its values, and dissolved the socialist ideology into a non-committal phraseology. Later on, it even abolished Socialism as a form of social organization. Erich Honecker, in particular, nurtured the philistine approach to lifestyle and outlook on the world, and offered consumerism, in a restricted version, comparable to that of the West, in exchange for political subservience, and a small cottage in exchange for the right to decide on one's own affairs.

GDR life thus became an arrangement, a *contrat social* of the cheap sort, from which the people firmly contracted out at the first opportunity. 'We pretend to work, they pretend to pay us', was a popular saying, expressing that arrangement. 'Freitag um eins, macht jeder seins' ('On Friday at noon, everyone is doing his own job') was another one, though the official working time lasted until five p.m. The inherent consumerism in an undersupplied society is illustrated by the policy of the authorities when the impending crisis became obvious in the early 1980s. At that time there was a substantial undercurrent in the population ready to restrict consumption and to make sacrifices for ecological and economic reforms. The rulers never tried to gain support from that movement; instead, they vigorously suppressed it and denounced it as a West-guided attempt to cheat the working classes out of their well-deserved reward. The overall result of the ensuing overstrain was an

economic as well as an ecological catastrophe that made any attempt
to reform socialism a hopeless venture.

Another outcome was a deeply rooted and widespread consumer
mentality in the population, which, however, was permanently
thwarted by comparison with the West. This state of frustration
produced in the last decade a paranoid obsession with unreal
aspirations that I will illustrate with some examples. But first let me
point out that it produced a second trait in the popular mentality,
namely 'my house is my castle and everything outside it is
Honecker's business, not mine': I mean a retreat into privacy and
disregard of the community to an extent that became massively self-
damaging. In the low-rise suburbs on the outskirts of Berlin, for
instance, the state-organized disposal of refuse, in particular of bulky
rubbish, did not function. So at night-time people dumped
discarded sofas and television sets, as well as stinking garbage, in
the woods or in the brook close by; and afterwards they would keep
getting annoyed about the sorry sight and smell of rotting trash
they experienced during their forest walks at the weekend. The
miserable state of public cleanliness finally made people furious
with their rulers, especially when they detected that they too had
behaved in the same way, retreating into housing estates
inaccessible to the public, but run by operating staff who took care
of the waste disposal, among other services. The opening of
Honecker's and the politbureau's settlement in Wandlitz late in
1989 contributed considerably to the toppling of the system,
although their luxury was modest compared with that of a well-to-
do pharmacist in a West German town.

Die Unwirklichkeit der Realität: this is how the ex-GDR sociologist
Wolfgang Engler has nicknamed that strange world of hallucination
which became the centre of the life of the East German population.
I have difficulty in translating the expression into English, perhaps
because the English-speaking peoples have escaped the
overwhelming influence of the philosopher Georg Friedrich Wilhelm
Hegel, who introduced a careful distinction between *Wirklichkeit* and
Realität. Reality is 'things' and other objects which just exist, while
Wirklichkeit has some actual, effective presence. East German people
lived in two worlds: during the day in a reality that they recognized
less and less as actual life. Most of their aspirations and
achievements, apart from very private ones, immediately lost their
fascination when being compared with the world into which they
emigrated every evening by switching on West German television.

This showed a world at the same time unreal and *wirklich* (effective). The citizen waited, yearned for ten years to get a *Trabant* car, decorating it like a jewellery box, giving it tender nicknames. But his pride was immediately reduced to disappointment when his West German cousin, with a one-day's entrance-visa into East Berlin, appeared with his *Opel* or *Ford* car. And with the accompanying condescension.

But not only in the sphere of consumer goods, even more so in the intellectual sphere. The Easterner barely squeezed traces of entertainment out of the newspaper *Neues Deutschland* and was desperately struggling to get hold of the latest edition of *Der Spiegel*. He had years to wait until some empathic soul risked and usually experienced pestering and confiscation by the border police, including the possible denial of an entry visa, by trying to smuggle a work by the philosopher Adorno as a gift into the workers' and peasants' paradise; while the only shreds of Western printed culture he could normally get hold of were deprecatingly annotated quotations in one of the brochures of the series *Kritik der bürgerlichen Philosophie*. To cut a long story short: the fascinating West was unattainable, unreal, but actual, while his own realm was worthless. I know of people who actively dismantled their professional careers in order to become released, for instance, from the all-embracing and absurd secrecy and security commitments, because this was a necessary condition for obtaining an exit permit to undertake a few days' private visit to the aunt of their mother-in-law in Cologne on the occasion of her 80th birthday.

Many inhabitants of that strangely unaccepted though real world were thus in a state of devotion to the West that contributed very much to the irresistible rush into the premature implementation of unification in 1990, but also to the similarly exaggerated disappointment in the years thereafter, when it became clear that what was being entered at any price after 45 years of exile was no paradise. As in a fairy-tale, the GDR citizens expected to be led into the king's castle to enjoy a life in precious clothes for the rest of their days. Reality turned out, quite naturally, to be different from that illusion.

But the inevitable frustration, which by now has sometimes taken ridiculous forms, reinforced another trait of East German mentality that had grown through the generations: authoritarianism and subservience accompanied by an expectation that the state has to take care of you. The co-founder of *Neuen Forums*, the New Forum movement, in 1989, Rolf Henrich, a lawyer living not far from Berlin, published in the late 1980s in the West a booklet that caused considerable annoyance to the GDR authorities. Its title was *Der vormundschaftliche Staat*, the tutelary state. The book describes quite aptly a population placed under guardianship. With hindsight and an acquired standard of comparison we can now realize that the late socialist state was heavily tutelary and authoritarian, but not bureaucratic, or at worst mildly so. We see now what a very large part of our vital affairs was settled by the state without any interference from our side. I could again tell stories about that tacit solicitude and the disappointment after release. People did not realize this. They were usually quite dissatisfied with their guardian state and made use of the first occasion in 1990 to get rid of it, but they transferred their expectations to the new Federal Republic and to Helmut Kohl, or whoever else would be assigned as their guardian. Full employment, wages fixed by the authorities, a basic supply of goods at low prices, exemption from taxation, a supply of housing at low rents, social and medical security, possibly at zero cost, professional qualifications served up in a well-prepared and easy programme, public law and order, revenge on the previous rulers, protection against competitors – everything is delegated to the state in Bonn and expected to be fulfilled by it. A subservient mentality combined with passivity: this is the heritage of two, and in the Soviet Union, four generations of state socialism which was responsible for everything and released us from planning ahead for our own futures. This tendency was reinforced after 1990: by a restorative programme conducted from above, trying to revitalize 'old values' of family, law and order. At the same time an extremely individualistic and hedonistic 'postmodernism' lifestyle poured into the society. Religion was reimposed on a profoundly pagan population by state authority: the automatic deduction of church tax by the state was re-introduced by law, provoking a mass exodus and mass alienation from the Churches that now presents a major threat to their continued existence. The introverted family role of women was grafted back into a society which in this particular respect was far more modern than the Federal Republic. Symbolic forms, like national identity, were over-emphasized in a society which for several generations had been weaned away from that idea. Democracy came as a formal rule to a population which was accustomed to retreat from public affairs and to denounce the public sphere as realm of political careerism and pomposity.

I could continue, but I think I have given you some impression of the mentality of the East Germans and of their difficulties of adjustment. My outlook? My recipe? Well, I am preaching cool composure and imperturbability. We will experience a very slow regeneration of the political sphere and of a non-political public domain. Self-assurance will gradually grow, together with a republican spirit. I can even see a positive aspect in the defiant support of the Party of Democratic Socialism to the annoyance of Herr Kohl in Bonn and Herr Waigel in Bavaria. Such stubbornness is preferable to the passive resignation that prevailed in the earlier years. A change in the political mentality will take a generation. But I see a ray of hope when looking at the younger generation. My three adult children are very self-assured, without post-socialist inferiority complex or obstinacy – they manage post-socialist life already much better than I do. What makes me uneasy about the younger generation, East as well West German, is the calm tolerance – a surface calm, to be sure – with which they accept the crisis of civilization that is certain to come. I am trying to arouse them whenever there is an opportunity. 'It is your future that is at stake', I say. 'Do not leave it to the decisions of the established powers-that-be. You become alert. Listen to the experience of my age group. We have kept an angry silence and have waited much too long. It was late when, in 1989, we finally detected that it is possible to shape our fate ourselves. We thought for nearly 30 years: 'It's impossible, we're powerless.' We had internalized the 17th of June in 1953, the Hungarian October of 1956, the outcome of the Prague spring in 1968, the bloody winter of Gdansk in 1970, the campaign of Jaruzelski against his own people in 1982. But gradually these recollections became a system of mere self-exculpation. In 1989 we learned how easily fundamental changes can be achieved, provided that we pull ourselves together and find a method of co-operative action.'

Listeners usually look at me with detached amusement when I am thus gesticulating wildly. I realize that I have to be patient until the wind of change blows once more. Perhaps still within the present century? My point of reference is 1989, not the lame time since.

Notes on Contributors

HERMANN GLASER is Professor for Cultural Studies at the Technical University of Berlin. He was Cultural Commissioner of the city of Nuremberg (1964–1990). As an author of many books on German history, cultural history and literature he is a member of the PEN.

His publications include *Kulturgeschichte der Bundesrepublik Deutschland*, 3 vols (1990); *Behagen und Unbehagen in der Kulturpolitik* (1992); *Bildungsbürgertum und Nationalsozialismus* (1993); *Industriekultur und Alltagsleben. Vom Biedermeier zur Postmoderne* (1994); *1945. Ein Lesebuch* (1995).

HORST ALBERT GLASER is Professor of General and Comparative Literature at the University of Essen. Visiting Fellowships include Università di Pisa, Università di Trieste, Universiteit van Amsterdam, University of Natal, South Africa and Universität Jena. He has published on the European literature of the last four centuries.

His publications include *Die Restauration des Schönen. Stifters 'Nachsommer'* (1965); *Das bürgerliche Rührstück* (1969); *Die utopische Insel* (1995). He is editor of the *Deutsche Literatur – eine Sozialgeschichte* (1982–1995); *Sexualästhetik der Literatur* (1970), *Goethe und die Natur* (1986); *Maschinenmenschen* (1988); *Gottfried Benn* (1989) and several other books on German and European literature.

REINER POMMERIN is Professor of Modern and Contemporary History at the University of Dresden. Visiting Fellowships include Harvard University, Universität Jena and St Antony's College, Oxford. He has published on the history of international relations in the last three centuries and on strategic studies.

His publications include *Das Dritte Reich und Lateinamerika. Die deutsche Politik gegenüber Süd- und Mittelamerika 1939–1942* (1977); *Sterilisierung der Rheinlandbastarde. Das Schicksal einer farbigen deutschen Minderheit 1918–1937* (1979); *Der Kaiser und Amerika. Die USA in der Politik der Reichsleitung 1890–1917* (1986); *Von Berlin nach Bonn. Die Alliierten, die Deutschen und die Hauptstadtfrage nach 1945* (1989); and, with Johannes Steinhoff, *Strategiewechsel. Bundesrepublik und Nuklearstrategie in der Ära Adenauer-Kennedy* (1992). He also edited *The American Impact on Postwar Germany* (1995).

JENS REICH is Professor of Bioinformatics at the Max Delbrueck Centre of Molecular Medicine in Berlin-Buch. He was active in the grass-roots democratic movement in former East Germany and was in 1989 one of the founders of new Forum group that contributed to toppling the communist regime. In 1990 he was a member of the GDR's last parliament that prepared the unification with the Federal Republic of Germany. He was a Visiting Fellow on European Affairs at Harvard University (1992). In 1994 he was one of the candidates for the presidency of the Federal Republic.

His publications (other than those in the field of bioinformatics) include *Rückkehr nach Europa* (1991; paperback 1993); *Die Intelligenz und die Macht* (1992); *Jens Reich im Gespräch* (1993). He is a regular contributor to *Die Zeit*.

THOMAS SIEVERTS is Professor of town planning and urban design at the Technical University of Darmstadt. He has a consulting firm in Bonn, whose main fields of activity are urban renewal, urban expansion and housing. He frequently acts as judge in architectural competitions and has acted as a consultant for many years for the city of Vienna. He has published widely in professional magazines and books. For the last five years he has been director of the International Building Exhibition *Emscher Park*, a workshop for the renewal of old industrial areas.

KURT SONTHEIMER is Professor emeritus at the University of Munich. He taught Political Science at the Free University of Berlin (1962–1969), and then at the Geschwister Scholl-Institut of Political Science at Munich University (1970–1993). He has published on recent German history and politics, mainly about the Federal Republic.

His publications include *Antidemokratisches Denken in der Weimarer Republik* (1962), *Thomas Mann und die Deutschen* (1961), *Grundzüge des politischen Systems der neuen Bundesrepublik* (16th edn, 1994), and *Die Adenauer-Ära* (1991).

ERNST VOLLRATH is Professor of Philosophy at the University of Cologne. He formerly held the positions of full professor (*professeur titulaire*) at the University of Dakar, Senegal (1967–1968) and of Professor and Theodor Heuss Professor at the Graduate Faculty of the New School for Social Research in New York City (1972–1976). He specializes in the field of Political Philosophy.

He has published almost one hundred essays (on Marx, Rosa Luxemburg, Max Weber, Heidegger, Critical Theory, Habermas, German *Staatsrechtslehre*, etc) and *Lenin und der Staat, Zum Begriff des Politischen bei Lenin* (1977); *Die Rekonstruktion der Politischen Urteilskraft* (1977); and *Grundlegung einer philosophischen Theorie des Politischen* (1987).

WOLFGANG WELSCH is Professor of Philosophy at the University of Magdeburg. Visiting Professorships include the University of Erlangen-Nuremberg, the Free University of Berlin, the Humboldt University of Berlin and Stanford University. In 1992 he received the Max Planck Research Award.

His main publications include *Aisthesis. Grundzüge und Perspektiven der Aristotelischen Sinneslehre* (1987); *Unsere postmoderne Moderne* (1987; English edition 1995); *Ästhetisches Denken* (1990; English edition 1996); *Vernunft. Die zeitgenössische Vernunftkritik und das Konzept der transversalen Vernunft* (1995). He has edited *Wege aus der Moderne. Schlüsseltexte der Postmoderne-Diskussion* (1988); *Die Aktualität des Ästhetischen* (1993); and, with Christine Pries, *Ästhetik im Widerstreit. Interventionen zum Werk von Jean-François Lyotard* (1991).

Suggestions for Further Reading

Manfred Abelein, *Die Kulturpolitik des Deutschen Reiches und die Bundesrepublik Deutschland. Ihre verfassungsrechtliche Entwicklung und ihre verfassungsrechtlichen Probleme*, Cologne – Opladen 1968.

Lothar Bickel, *Kultur*, Zurich 1956.

Lothar Bossle, *Deutschland als Kulturstaat*, Paderborn 1993.

Helmut Brackert and Fritz Wefelmeiyer, *Naturplan und Verfallskritik: Zu Begriff und Geschichte der Kultur*, Frankfurt am Main 1984.

Helmut Brackert and Fritz Wefelmeyer, *Kultur: Bestimmungen im 20. Jahrhundert*, Frankfurt am Main 1990.

Helmut Engler, 'Die Kulturhoheit der deutschen Länder im System der EG', *Politische Studien* 42, July/August 1991, 345–54.

Johann Ernst, *Illustrierte deutsche Kulturgeschichte der letzten hundert Jahre*, Munich 1983.

Felix Gilbert, *History – Politics or Culture?. . . Geschichte – Politik oder Kultur. Rückblick auf einen klassischen Konflikt*, Frankfurt 1992.

Hermann Glaser and Karl Heinz Stahl, *Bürgerrecht Kultur*, Frankfurt am Main – Berlin – Vienna 1983.

Hermann Glaser, *Kulturgeschichte der Bundesrepublik Deutschland*, 3 vols, Munich 1985–1989.

Hermann Glaser, *The Rubble Years: The Cultural Roots of Postwar Germany*, New York 1986.

Hermann Glaser, *Kleine Kulturgeschichte der Bundesrepublik Deutschland, 1945–1989*, Munich 1991.

Hermann Glaser, 'Kultur und Gesellschaft in der Bundesrepublik', *Aus Politik und Zeitgeschichte* 1991, Vol. 1/2, 3–15.

Hermann Glaser, *1945. Ein Lesebuch*, Frankfurt am Main 1995.

Horst Albert Glaser (ed.), *Deutsche Literatur – eine Sozialgeschichte*, Reinbek, 1982–1995.

Horst Albert Glaser (ed.), *Maschinenmenschen*, Frankfurt am Main 1988.

Joachim-Rüdiger Groth, *Widersprüche. Literatur und Politik in der DDR 1949–1989*, Berne – Berlin – Frankfurt am Main 1994.

Erna Heckel, *Kulturpolitik in der Bundesrepublik von 1949 bis zur Gegenwart*, Cologne 1987.

Jost Hermand, *Kultur im Wiederaufbau. Die Bundesrepublik Deutschland 1945–1965*, Munich 1986.

Jost Hermand, *Die Kultur der Bundesrepublik Deutschland 1965–85*, Munich 1988.

Hilmar Hoffmann, *Kultur für alle. Perspektiven und Modelle*, Frankfurt am Main 1979.

Hilmar Hoffmann, *Kultur für morgen*, Frankfurt am Main 1985.

Marlies Hummel and Karl-Heinz Brodbeck, *Längerfristige Wechselwirkungen zwischen kultureller und wirtschaftlicher Entwicklung*, Berlin 1991.

Humphreys, P. J., *Media and Media Policy in West Germany. Press and Broadcasting since 1945*, Oxford 1990.

Manfred Jäger, *Kultur und Politik in der DDR 1945–1990*, Cologne 1995.

Konrad Jarausch, *Geschichtswissenschaft vor 2000. Perspektiven der Historiographiegeschichte, Geschichtstheorie, Sozial- und Kulturgeschichte. Festschrift für Georg Iggers zum 65. Geburtstag*, Hagen 1991.

Roger Manvell and Heinrich Fraenkel, *The German Cinema*, London 1971.

Reiner Pommerin, 'Die Architektur der zweiten Republik: Ausdruck eines demokratischen Staatswesens', *Der Architekt* 10, 1989, 487–92.

Reiner Pommerin (ed.), *The American Impact on Postwar Germany*, Providence – Oxford 1995.

Nicholas Pronay and Keith Wilson, *The Political Re-Education of Germany and her Allies After World War II*, London 1985.

Jens Reich, *Rückkehr nach Europa*, Munich 1991.

Jens Reich, *Die Intelligenz und die Macht*, Berlin 1992.

Jens Reich, *Jens Reich im Gespräch*, Munich 1993.

Günther Rüther (ed.), *Kulturbetrieb und Literatur in der DDR*, Cologne 1987.

Günther Rüther, *'Greif zur Feder Kumpel'. Schriftsteller, Literatur und Politik in der DDR 1949–1990*, Dusseldorf 1991.

Helmut Schelsky, *Die Arbeit tun die anderen. Klassenkampf und Priesterherrschaft der Intellektuellen*, Opladen 1975.

Wolfram Schlenker, *Das kulturelle Erbe in der DDR: gesellschaftliche Entwicklung und Kulturpolitik 1945–1965*, Stuttgart 1977.

Louise Schorn-Schütte, *Karl Lamprecht. Kulturgeschichtsschreibung zwischen Wissenschaft und Politik*, Göttingen 1984.

Thomas Sieverts and Karl Ganser, 'Vom Aufbaustab Speer bis zu

Internationalen Bauausstellung Emscher Park und darüber hinaus – Planungskulturen in der Bundesrepublik Deutschland', *Dokumente und Informationen Schweizer Planer*, 115, October 1993, 31–7.

Kurt Sontheimer, *Der Überdruß an der Demokratie. Neue Linke und alte Rechte. Unterschiede und Gemeinsamkeiten*, Cologne 1970.

Kurt Sontheimer, *Das Elend unserer Intellektuellen. Linke Theorie in der Bundesrepublik Deutschland*, Hamburg 1976.

Kurt Sontheimer, *Die verunsicherte Republik*, Munich 1979.

Franz Steinbacher, *Kultur, Begriff, Theorie, Funktion*, Stuttgart 1976.

Georg Steinhausen, *Geschichte der deutschen Kultur*, Leipzig 1929.

Joachim Streisand, *Kulturgeschichte der DDR: Studien zu ihren historischen Grundlagen und ihren Entwicklungsetappen*, Berlin 1981.

Hans Vogt, *Neue Musik nach 1945*, Stuttgart 1972.

Ernst Vollrath, *Lenin und der Staat. Zum Begriff des Politischen bei Lenin*, Wuppertal 1970.

Ernst Vollrath, *Die Rekonstruktion der politischen Urteilskraft*, Stuttgart 1977.

Ernst Vollrath, *Grundlegung einer Philosophie des Politischen*, Würzburg 1987.

Wolfgang Welsch, *Our Postmodern Modern*, New Brunswick, NJ, 1995.

Wolfgang Welsch, *Vernunft: Die zeitgenössische Vernunftkritik und das Konzept der transversalen Vernunft*, Frankfurt am Main, 1995.

Arthur Williams, *Broadcasting and Democracy in West Germany*, Bradford – London 1976.

Heide Wunder, *Kulturgeschichte, Mentalitätengeschichte, Historische Anthropologie*, in Richard van Dülmen (ed.), *Fischer Lexikon Geschichte*, Frankfurt am Main 1990, pp. 65–86.